D0335637

WONDERCRUMP POETRY!

WONDERCRUMP POETRY!

The best children's poems
from the
Roald Dahl
Poetry Competition,
1994

Edited by Jennifer Curry

RED FOX

A Red Fox Book

Published by Random House Children's Books
20 Vauxhall Bridge Road, London SW1V 2SA

A division of Random House UK Ltd
London Melbourne Sydney Auckland
Johannesburg and agencies throughout the world

Text © Random House Children's Books 1994
Designed by Ness Wood

1 3 5 7 9 10 8 6 4 2

Red Fox edition 1994

This book is sold subject to the condition that it shall not, by way of
trade or otherwise, be lent, resold, hired out, or otherwise circulated
without the publisher's prior consent in any form of binding or cover
other than that in which it is published and without a similar
condition including this condition being imposed on the subsequent
purchaser.

Set in Janson by SX Composing, Rayleigh, Essex
Printed and bound in Great Britain by
Cox & Wyman Ltd, Reading, Berkshire.

RANDOM HOUSE UK Limited Reg. No. 954009

ISBN 0 09 930328 0

Contents

Poetic Justice

When I was asked to write the foreword to this wonderful book I accepted with fear and trepidation because I know nothing about poetry. So why, you ask, did I accept? Well, for three reasons. Firstly, I was Roald's wife and I would never let him down. Secondly, I started the Roald Dahl Foundation and no way could I let it down. But thirdly, my main reason was I realised that perhaps I was the perfect person for the task as I think this book is about learning to love reading and writing poetry.

So I started by looking up the definition of the word poetry in the Oxford Dictionary. 'Literature in metrical form; verse.' Well, I thought that sounded rather boring until I noticed the definition for poetic licence above: 'Justifiable departure from conventional rules of form, fact, logic etc as in poetry', and I thought that sounded much more fun. Then I looked up poet. It said 'A person with great imagination and creativity'. It was then I wished I was a poet.

Roald always loved poetry and encouraged me to read it. I would often find little rhymes written by him on my desk. He was constantly sending them to teachers and children all over the world. How proud he would be of this book. If he was alive he would congratulate all the thousands of children who entered this competition and especially the ones in the pages of this book. He would call them all WONDERCRUMPS.

> "As I grow old and just a trifle frayed
> It's nice to know that sometimes I have made
> You children and occasionally the staff
> Stop work and have instead a little laugh."

I hope the poets all had as much fun writing their poems as he had writing his. I congratulate them all.

Felicity Dahl.

FIRST WORDS...

Here I have a blank piece of paper

Here I have a blank piece of paper
And my mind is blank too.
What I'm trying to say
Is how hard I find it to write.
I can't seem to get started.
James has written four pages already;
An hour has gone and I've nothing to show for it.
My brain is still trying to think
But by the time my ideas
Reach my hand,
They have all gone
Like leaves blown from the trees in Autumn.
Numbers flow freely from my pen
But words are a mystery.
I don't seem to have much to say
And it takes all the time in the world to say it.
My paper is empty
Like a bare room,
Silent as sleeping children.

Graham Ashman (8)
Combs Ford C.P. School
Stowmarket, Suffolk

LAUGHING NOTES

Poems of delight

Cockling

We climbed down
The green, slimy ladders,
Until our feet
Touched . . .
The soft wet sand,
To sink slightly.
On the surface
Were lugworm trails,
Like mounds of spaghetti.
Near the sea,
We started raking.
Cockles popped up
Like peas in hot bubbling water.
We washed them
In little pools
That the sea had left behind.
Back in the caravan
Into the saucepan they went,
Into boiling water.
After a while . . .
Pop! Pop! Pop! Pop!

As the cockles parted
From their ridged shells,
Leaving the pebble-like insides
With fringed yellow edges.
They hit the saucepan sides,
Ready to cool down.
And be eaten.

Charlotte Baldry (13)
Halesworth Middle School
Halesworth, Suffolk

At the seaside

The sea sounded like thunder
The waves were a hundred hungry white dolphins
As they reached the pebbled shore.
Then everything was calm.

James Stephen Matthews (5)
Pontrhydyrun, Gwent

My cave

I listen as I walk through
my cave and I hear the
sea behind me.
I find pebbles and shells
in the darkness of my cave,
and driftwood and seaweed
in different colours.
I love my cave as I explore new things.

Emma Quémard (7)
Plat Douet School
St Saviour, Jersey

The sea and the seagull

No fish today
Because you had ten yesterday
I know you like them
You're not allowed
I'll make you a deal
Two fish a day

Alex Agar (7)
Saltburn Primary School
Saltburn, Cleveland

What did the sea say to the sandcastle?

He said, with a crash,
I'll smash you down to atoms
You'll fall to slippy sludge
I'm going to let everything knock you down
And I'll get crabs to nip at you
Now you are finished
Triton's honour

David Scales (7)
Saltburn Primary School
Saltburn, Cleveland

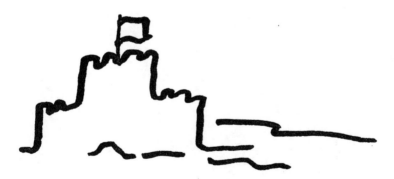

Happiness is.

Jumping over the waves
Playing with my friends
My teacher being pleased with me.
Giving presents to each other
Drawing a picture
Having a baby
When everybody else is happy

Hannah Gormley (6)
Trelales Primary School
Bridgend, Mid Glamorgan

Dear Pencilcase

Dear Pencilcase,
    Please let me out,
    I'm sore and bruised and it hurts me to shout.
    My lead is broken,
    My friends are gone,
    Only their shavings linger on.
    My rubber crumbles,
    My back is sore,
    My paintwork chipped, I can't take much more!
    So please dear Pencilcase don't let this be,
    Let me have freedom,
    Let me be free!
             Lots of love and kisses too,
             Yours sincerely
               Pencil (blue)
               x x x

             Alexandra Higbee (11)
              Saint Felix School
              Southwold, Suffolk

The history teacher

He comes chug, chug, chugging to school on his moped,
"L" plates on the back,
He zooms along the corridor,
mowing boys down who haven't jumped out of the way!
Office bound,
to type the daily calendar.
His rusty old sneeze
spurts out clouds of dust.
His beard, containing yesterday's cornflakes,
looks like it belongs to Henry VIII.
Hairstyle of Richard I,
temper of Attila the Hun,
and eyes as blue as the ocean sailed on by Columbus in
    1492.
His clothes are like something worn by King Alfred.
His jumpers are an explosion
and his ties are as interesting as the white lines down the
middle of the road!
His faithful lazy old dog,
snores in an archaeology of speech.

Memorable lessons on the Battle of Jutland,
when the board marker pen turns into a missile and goes
flying towards . . .
George Brown, his favourite target.
And when he taught the Black Hole of Calcutta,
cramming a class of fourteen into his musty cupboard.
THIS IS THE HISTORY TEACHER.

Paul West (11)
Orwell Park School,
Ipswich, Suffolk

The playground

Noisy children dashing about, getting their breaks.
The wind is blowing.
It is nearly dinnertime.
The birds are singing.
Somebody's crying.
The ball is going bounce, bounce, bounce.
The skipping rope is going whoop, whoop, whoop.
Some boys are playing football.
Bang, bang, thud against the wall.
The boys are shouting goal, goal, goal.
It's in-time.

Jemma Matthews (7)
Blisland C.P. School
Blisland, Cornwall

Bikes

We are on our bikes, whizzing along,
Pedalling to the shops to buy some sweets and stickers.

We went to the park, like we are on a racing track,
Whizzing along, our hair is blowing in the wind.

Then we go home.

Christopher Foy and Scott Pritchett (7/6)
Stamshaw First School
Stamshaw, Portsmouth

Fireworks

Fireworks are like flowers:
Flowers in towers.
Fireworks are like stars in the dark sky.

Kimberley Underwood (7)
Herbert Morrison Primary School
Stockwell, South London

Rugby match

Rugby's a rough team game
Not for cissies
Not for the tame.
Push and shove
Chase the ball
Into the muck you may fall.
In the scrum
Some bloke's bum
Next to your face
Hope he's a chum.
Blood and tears
Cauliflower ears
Scream and shout
Broken snout
Rushing forward
Falling floorward
Wingers, props
Stinky socks.
Changing room
Nice hot shower
Home for tea
In less than an hour.

John Kunes (11)
Hitchin Boys School
Hitchin, Herts

Hair

Hair is brill, hair is brill
Curly hair, Straight hair
Brown hair, Yellow hair
Long hair, Short hair
Parted hair, Messy hair
Hair on chests, hair under arms
Hair on heads, no hair, lots of hair
Hair under noses
Hair today . . .

                gone tomorrow.

Aaron Lockwood (9)
Stowmarket Middle School
Stowmarket, Suffolk

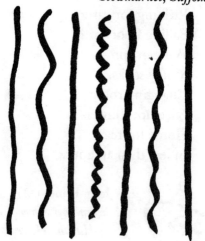

Having my hair cut

It tickles when Donna sprays
my hair with water.
It feels like rain falling.
It is cold like ice.
The way the scissors go across
my hair makes me excited.
I wait to see if I'm somebody new.

I look in the mirror
I look in the mirror
I look again
I can't help it.

A stranger looks back at me.
She's smiling.
I know the smile.

Ellen Coffey (6)
Handford Hall Primary School
Ipswich
(Age Category Winner

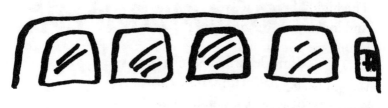

"Are we nearly there yet?"

We got on the coach for London,
Hoping we'd see the tower,
We sat on the coach for ages,
We sat on the coach for hours.

We eventually got to cold Trafalgar Square,
Our hands were all a quiver,
We ate our lunch on the banks of the Thames,
But Tom's floated off down the river.

We were all very sensible,
But Jake was a bit of a danger,
It was great strolling up Downing Street,
And having tea and buns with John Major.

We walked past 'Planet Hollywood',
And saw a rather suspicious barman,
We had great fun in the British Museum,
And a long chat with Tutankhamun.

We saw Nelson on his column,

The highlight of the day,
And looking at Buckingham Palace,
I think we got a wave.

We got back on the coach for home,
Saying "Cheerio" to Big Ben,
But the phrase that was asked throughout the coach was,
"Are we nearly there yet?" again . . . and again and . . .
   again.

Lucie Davis (11)
St John's C. of E. Middle School
Blakebrook, Kidderminster

Cold like ice

Cold like ice and hot like fire
giving you a shock like a plug and wire
because people go crazy when the mic's in my hand
I like robocop
and you're a regular man
These rhymes are mine and not stolen

The mic that I'm holding
You told some rhymes that are weak so I was rolling
around on the ground because it was so funny
don't call me honey you'll never make no money.
My rhymes are written fresh and never bitten
I'm standing and you're sitting
you hear me and then you're quittin'
You're out of the game nobody knows your name
And your claim to fame is that you show no shame
New York to Kilburn City yes coast to coast and I am
busting mc like ghostbuster does ghost
I'm willing and able
to rock the mic and turntable
if I'm not on tour and home watching cable
I made my name so I can let them know
so on your marks get set and here we go
I make the crowd go insane don't use cocaine
I like to travel a lot because I travel by airplane
sitting by the window talking to a bimbo
Taking you off balance like your life was in limbo
yo I'm hard to handle hotter than a candle
sloppy like Oscar but knees like Tony Randall
my rhymes are inconceivable
it's unbelievable
it's easy to me but to you it's unachievable
This is a throwdown forget about the lowdown
Live from St Augustine for a hip hop showdown
my lip service makes you nervous
don't play dumb because you know that you deserve this
renegade, rebel, rocking bass rocking treble

taking hip hop to your mind and level
elevating hip hop
let me make a pit stop go tell your friends about the
champ they call nonstop.

Junior Hannouch (13)
St Augustine's School
North London

The songbird

I was bored,
Getting tired.
Not really interested.

The conductor drew up his baton,
Puffed out his chest.

I glanced at my programme;
Bow-tie after bow-tie was straightened.
Black silk rustled importantly.
Efficiently.

Flute poised ready to dance.
Violin under powdered chin.
Trumpets glint.

WONDERCRUMP POETRY!   27

Then the songbird swooped
Laughing notes soared through my mind.
Violins teased. I could smell dusty wood and ancient rosin.
Flutes darted every place
Doubling up, whispering secrets.
Oboes told of tragedy,
Sent a shiver down my spine.
The whole sound a massive waterfall.

I clench my fingers, feeling I will hit the bottom
But the spirit songbird flies on.

Elisabeth Williamson (13)
Coleraine High School
Coleraine, N. Ireland

MA IS CHOPPING ONIONS

Poems of home and family

My mum likes to watch TV

My Mum likes to watch TV.
She doesn't like to make the tea.
So John, Geoffrey, and me have to
make our own you see.
And so has our poor dear Daddy.

Claire Kwateng (6)
St Mary's Infant School
Bedford Park, Croydon

My mummy

I love my mummy
Because she feeds my tummy
And my tummy loves my mummy!

Michelle Rysdale (5)
Seven Stars County Infant School
Leyland, Preston

Let's make the Christmas cake

"Come and make the Christmas cake,"
Mummy calls to us all.
Two children rush to the kitchen
Scattering their books and their balls
Put in the butter, put in the sugar
Mix around, mix around.
Beat the eggs until it foams,
Make the air bubbles go POP!
Flour falls on the mixture
Like snowflakes on the ground.
Add the glistening fruit soaked in brandy.
Mix around, mix around.
Hands eager to touch
The sloppy brown mixture.
"I want a taste"
"Leave some for me"
Licking lips edge to the bowl
As Mummy scoops the mixture out,

Children dive to the bowl
Gooey hands, smeared moustachey faces.
    "Yum, yum," they chorus,
    "Delicious,"
    "WE WANT SOME MORE!"
"Well wait till Christmas Day!"

> Naomi Benger (7)
> *Hockliffe, Beds.*

Fireworks

Fireworks give me a fright
My Dad said, "Don't be frightened of the fireworks.
They are as pretty as a rainbow."

> Sophie Denne (6)
> *Christ Church Infant School*
> *Virginia Water, Surrey*

Kitchen noises

Pots and pans bashing
Plates go crashing.
Oven is humming
While washing is drumming.
Taps dripping, scissors snipping.
Cupboards banging
Kitchen door slamming.
Sink gushing
Potato mashing.
Kettle singing
Spoon clinking.
But the thing I like most, even more than toast,
IS . . .
        Mum's bolognaise.

Matthew Hinton (6)
Greasby Infants School
Greasby, Wirral

Stowey Mill

Once on the wall the cabinet's glass
sparkled with sunlight.
Now the ivy spreads,
eating into the mortar
with its powerful stems,
nothing to stand in its way.
In the corner the old copper sat
bubbling and simmering,
waiting for Pa's oil-stained shirts.
Now weeds grow there as tall as me.
A tree towers taller
thar the crumbling walls,
spreading its branches
to roof the old kitchen.
I can remember the herbs that hung
in rows of six and seven above the window.
Now the window has given in
to the weight of the wall above,
and all sorts of fungi grow
orange, brown and yellow.
Once in the centre of the room,
newly scrubbed, a long pine table gleamed.
I can remember it well.
If I close my eyes
I can see us all:
my brother, my sister, my pa and ma.
There's a comforting smell of roast chicken

wafting around the room,
and a sound like potatoes boiling over.
I go over to where Ma is chopping onions
with her razor-sharp knife.
I can feel my eyes fill like the leat
when Pa opens the sluice-gate.
I brush away my tears and look around.
Is this where my father stood,
where now the maggots seethe?
Is this where my mother cooked,
where the leaves pile high?
Is this where my sister trudged
red-faced up to school?
Is this where the child played
on the old flagstone floor?

Sarah Beth Lyle (10)
Cutcombe, Somerset

The soggy cornflake

On a draining board,
In a sunshiney kitchen,
In a bright yellow bowl,
One single, solitary, soggy cornflake sits,
The owner of the bowl forgot about it.
I don't think that they were saving it for later,
Or now, or never.
It sits there, clinging to the side of the bowl,
absorbing the leftover milk.
Sucking it in, not spitting it out.
Maybe the milk is its only friend,
Maybe not.
The other cornflakes,
In the brightly coloured Kelloggs box,
Have gone, forever perhaps,
I doubt very much that they'll be seen again,
Not by this single, solitary, soggy cornflake anyway.

Amy Powell (14)
Dillwyn Llewellyn Comprehensive School
Cockett

Wash day

Sunday night
Clothes soaked
Monday morning
It's very hard work
Up down
Round and round
Goes the dolly
Soapy white bubbles
It's very hard work
Scrub, scrub, scrub
Goes the scrubbing board
It's very hard work
Round and round goes the mangle
It's very hard work
Clothes on line
It's very hard work
Glowing fire
Spit on iron
It's very hard work

Catherine Prew (7)
Binfield C. of E. Primary School
Bracknell, Berks

To Anyone

Will anyone listen?
Is anyone there?
I've got some secrets
I've been longing to share
I've just had my hair cut
A day or two ago,
But at the moment
My
   Dad
      Doesn't
         Know!

Laura Lewarne (10)
Hill View School
Banbury, Oxon

Laser gun

Behind a door you hear a noise,
Of children playing with their toys.
ZAP! POW! I shot your head!
NO! You were already dead.
I was not!
You were too!

I'm telling Dad of you!
Go ahead, make my day,
You always cry anyway!
I do not!
You do too!
Anyway, I need the loo.
Daddy, Daddy, hear what he said;
He wouldn't admit to being dead!
Oh, that's nice dear,
Having fun,
Playing with your laser gun!

Philip Cooper (11)
Thorpe St Andrew School
Thorpe St Andrew, Norwich
(School of the Year)

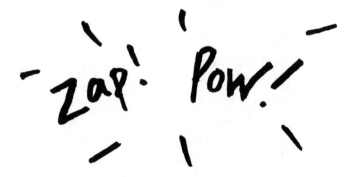

To my brother

Once we would sit
Together,
In the same bath,
Idly playing
In the lukewarm water.
But somewhere
Along that childhood road
I got left behind.
You had your friends;
I had mine.
Then, different people,
Strangers,
We would meet in the playground
And you'd turn away.
Then, last summer at Stony Cove
We dived
And suddenly,
Once again, we were
Together,
Idly playing
In the lukewarm water.

Saffron Barnes (14)
Debenham High School
Stowmarket, Suffolk

My brother and his chocs

My brother always wanted to go into space
to eat all the chocs
Mars,
Galaxy,
and of course the Milky Way.
But I tried to explain they were planets
but he didn't care what I said.
So he got into a spaceship
I don't know where he found it
He came back in a year or two
as fat as a pig and that was fat.
He said it was fun
Gee whizz, oh my moon and stars!
He said you ain't seen nothing yet
as he showed me what he had brought back.
It was a little pet alien
Yuk! Gross!
I ran 5-6 miles away
and guess what, I never saw my brother again.

Philippa Murray (9)
Fernwood Junior School
Wollaton, Nottingham

Anna

Anna is my sister
She pulls bananas out
She eats them with their skins on
And Fergle runs about.

Michaela Durbacz (4)
Brent Knoll Primary School
Highbridge, Somerset

My sister

My youngest sister is a pain,
She's so naughty again and again.
Every morning she is the same,
And what is worse I get the blame.
It is so sad, I just can't win,
'Cos after all she is my TWIN!!

My Dad says "I'll sort her out,"
But all he does is shout and shout.
But shouting doesn't do the trick,
It isn't fair it makes me sick.
It's such a crime, "Oh! What a sin"
Please, oh please *DON'T* HAVE A TWIN!!

Lisa Tilbury (12)
Sir William Robertson High School
Welbourn, Lincoln

I don't know why I cried (A sister leaving home)

The enormity of it all filled our house
Our own little world, exclusive to us.
Nothing else mattered, nothing else existed.
Everything melodramatic, out of proportion
Yet sincere and heart-felt.

I don't remember how it felt
Indescribable — a void of nothingness.
Uncontrollable grief appearing from nowhere,
Unexpected.
An eternal spring
Welling up, bubbling and overflowing.

I don't know why I cried,
But I cried,
Clutching her, making up for all the times
I'd turned her away.

But that wasn't enough. Never enough.
A sudden explosion of grief,
A grief of regret?

Had I enjoyed her as much as I should?
An end of an era?
Nothing stays the same.

I can't believe this is happening
At least, it isn't happening to me and my sister,
Like a bad dream. Occurring
And re-occurring.
Disbelief, hurt, uncertainty.
Love.
It was always expected,
Yet distant on the horizon.
She'll be back a different person.
A different friend.

Jenni Cator (16)
Thorpe St Andrew School
Norwich
(Age Category Winner)
(School of the Year Award)

A grandmother's story

I may be old,
But there's lots I do,
I walk and talk,
And tie my shoe.

I knit and sew,
And even drive,
These things I do
To stay alive.

I go for walks,
I watch TV,
To sit and moan,
That's just not me.
I can read,
And I can write.
To cuddle my grandchildren,
That's my delight.

Children come and go to school,
Do what they're told,
Follow the rule,
I am old,
I do what I like,
Follow no rules,
Even ride my bike.

I go to town,
Give in my book,
Collect the money,
Go home and cook.
Don't have to work
To earn a living,
I even have money
Left for giving.

To be old is not too bad,
In fact, it is quite good.
I can be bold,
I can be rude.
No one to scold,
Or tell me to go,
I'll do my own thing,
Blow rain or snow.

Bernadette Deehan (10)
St Patrick's Primary School
Dunnabanagh, Strabane

Grandmother

Grandmother sings
but doesn't swing.
Grandmother cooks
But doesn't fix hooks
and she does do a poo
but she doesn't go "wooo".
Will she do a Winnie the Pooh?
Will she win a race?
She is full of grace.

Jenny Edmunds (4)
Crewkerne, Somerset

Grandad

He bends
and digs the earthy soil,
his back creaking
like the door from the old attic.
The soil rolls over, like a playful dog,
to expose naked worms,
blind to the world.
The watering can
Sprays yet another generation of roses,
sprinkling on their petals,
and then,
is laid to rest
in the murky greenhouse.
Grandad hobbles,
painfully,
into the warm house
and settles down by the flickering flames
of the log fire.
He fits his glasses carefully
to the tip of his nose.
And starts to read.
His shining eyes
struggle to catch each word
as it passes under his nose,

while his mind thinks nothing much at all.
As darkness descends,
Grandad lifts his tired body to a more comfortable
        position
and settles down to his walnut whip.

Anna Elizabeth Rochead (13)
Halesworth Middle School
Halesworth, Suffolk

A poem about home

Home is a place where the dishonesty and badness
dies at the gates.
Where my brotherhood comes back and freedom does not
hide in the dust.
Home is where work is forgotten and love is at hand,
Where your heartbeat can wrap around you and you sleep
without disturbance from your friends,
where you are accepted as bad or good by the comfort and
family of your home.
When there is darkness and rain in this lonely world
there is only one place that accepts you:
that is your home.

Manmeet Singh (13)
St Nicholas School
Harlow, Essex

If I moved house!

If I moved house I'd take:
The times we canoe in the field when it floods,
my gerbil's grave
and the sound of the stream.

I wouldn't take:
the cat next door,
or the man next door.
They make noises in the night.

I'd take:
The mossy greenhouse
and the helicopter seeds,
the sheep making noises behind the house
and the sycamore tree I climb in.

I wouldn't take:
The smoke from next door when she has a fire.
or the alarm that goes off when Mum burns the cooking.

But I would take:
The weeping willow that hangs over the stream.

Nicola Brophy (10)
Etchingham CE Primary School
Etchingham, East Sussex

THE SUN IS A LOLLY

Poems about the natural world

The sheep

In the morning early
The steam
Rises
From the cold dewy ground.

The brown and white collie
Gathers the sheep
At my
Command.

He trots behind
The slow dozy sheep
Like a bird dodging
The trees.

Thomas Cleave (10)
Landscove C. of E. Primary School
Newton Abbot, Devon
(Roald Dahl Wondercrump School Award)

A frosty morning

The grass is like a floured floor
Snowy frosty wet and cold,

Under the shadows of the tree
There's white delicate frost

The grass is white
The leaves are speckled.

Matthew Watkins (7)
Garth Junior School
Garth, Maesteg

The falling leaf

A tiny leaf
fell
off my apple tree.
Gently
falling
from side to side.
Softly, safely
floating by.
It was

just like
the leaf
was
falling
in a
dream.
Then
the leaf
slowly
landed
on the
grass.

James Lefrere (7)
Great Linford Combined School
Great Linford, Milton Keynes

Reg and his veg

A wildlife gardener named Reg
Grew a haven of meadow and hedge.
The birds ate the bugs
The frogs ate the slugs
And Reg ate the organic veg.

Samantha Davies (12)
Churchfields High School
West Bromwich

The waterfall

Like leaves
Coming off a tree
The water drops
And tumbles.
It roars and smashes
It bounces back
And swirls in circles.

Jenny Clayden (7)
St David's R.C. Primary School
Newport, Gwent

Bubbles

Bubbles bounce
Up and down
Bubbles slippy
Bubbles delicate
Lighter than air
Each bursts
Smooth and colourful

Aaron Davies (6)
Castleton C.P. School
Whitby, N. Yorks

A gift returned

A child crouches on the bank
and watches the still grey water.
He lifts a stone and rubs off the dirt
until it sparkles in the winter light—
He holds it up high to the sky
displaying his beautiful gift
then draws it back and casts it out.
He shuts his eyes and breathes.
The stone flies like a bird set free
then plummets to the grey pool—
its haunting, hollow noise sounds
deep in the boy's soul.
A delicate glimmering ripple forms
and silently moves and grows
its colours changing smoothly in the greyness.
The magical movement reaches the boy
just as his grey eyes open.
The water returns to its stillness
but the light and magic is left
in the eyes of the small boy.
His gift has been returned.

Rosanne Flynn (14)
North London
(Poet of the Year)

The rain poem

Rain falls
Like little diamonds
On the ground.

Rain looks
Like little beetles
Bouncing up and down.

Rain sounds
Like little ants
Landing on the window.

Vicky Slight (7)
St David's R.C. Primary School
Newport, Gwent
(Age category winner)

Rain

Dribbling down my windowpane,
Oh no! It can't be, but yes it's rain
Puddles are forming in the street
If you don't avoid them, you'll get wet feet
As the rain gets heavier, people start to moan:
"If you go outside, you'll get soaked to the bone!"
It carries on as people go to their beds
But the pitter-patter stays in their heads.
When morning comes it's still tipping down
People are preparing in the country and town.
Out with the umbrellas, macs and wellies
"Quick, it's the weather forecast, switch on the telly."
A few days later the outlook is bleak
It seems that the rain has got to its peak
The road's a river and the pavement's a stream
I wish I could pinch myself and find it's all a dream
The water's neck-high so we've built a boat.
As we sail into the street I hope we'll stay afloat.
But the water pours in so I bale out with a jug
Suddenly I spot something, is it . . . yes it's a plug!
I swim down to pull it out but it's hard to budge
Using all my strength I pull it out. It comes out with a
   spludge!

The water gurgles, swooshes and is sucked away
Everyone lets out a huge "Hooray!"
Using towels and hairdryers we've dried up the city.
Actually I rather liked all that water – to drain it was a pity.

P.S. I am writing this in hiding, just in case anyone finds
out who left the plug in in the first place!

Daniel Williamson (11)
Thorpe St Andrew School
Norwich
(School of the Year)

Red alert

The siren goes. The panic is on.
The gushing of the water — splish splash splosh.
The water coming through the door.
Screaming. The worrying. The whistling of the wind.
Bang bang the window is broken.
Running up the stairs. I forgot the nappies.
What about the pets? My heart's beating even faster.
Panic everywhere. Oh no, I forgot the cat.
I will go and get it. No. I have got it. Look!
My heart's beating even faster.
Have we got everything? Yes. Oh good. I'm glad.
That's one less thing to worry about.

Are the children OK? Yes they're fine. They're fast asleep.
Good.
Whistling and whining.
Howling and groaning goes the wind.
The rain is still making these sounds.
Listen to it rushing, gushing, splashing,
gurgling, splashing.
I hope it's not going to get higher.
My heart's beating even faster than last time.
Phew, it's over. Everyone OK?
"Yes Mum," said the children.

Daniel Hawes (8)
Millfield C.P. School
North Walsham

The sun

The sun is a lolly
Nobody buys.
The sun is a yo-yo
That burns the string.
The sun is a ball
Rolling in space.

Mark Langley (7)
Greasby Infants School
Greasby, Wirral

Fog

I am the night when the fog horn will blow,
I am the night when no-one can see.
I am the night that makes cars go slow,
Everyone fears me.

I am the morning when mist hangs dense,
I am the morning when people drink tea
and look outside to see that I am immense,
Everyone fears me.

But when the wind starts to blow,
I begin to see.
That the wind will make me go,
and I am afraid.

Fahad Shahid Sayood (11)
Durston House School
Ealing, London

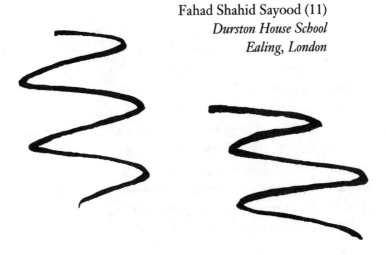

Vesuvius – tears of fire

Fires burned from hell all around me,
Great towering black clouds in a sky
Full of crimson, amber and gold
Dyeing all heaven and slow to fade.
Outside: people running, screaming, shouting
Like bees demented,
Wildly swarming around one honey-comb,
Clear, golden, fatal honey oozing through.
The bright, glittering, flashing red lava
Flowing past every crack in the city,
Like poisoned water from a broken cistern
Trickling into deep, menacing shadows
Causing complete destruction.
Inside: great columns crashing,
Huge shocks shaking the whole earth.
Beside me lay my mother.
Flamelight flickering on her pure sapphire dress,
The blood of her wound, as bright as a ruby gem.
Her eyes seemed to glitter with tears of fire
Beneath the glowing sky.
Pumice dust floors sliced with immense cracks,
Tongues of flames savagely licking through them.
Her sapphire dress had little folds full of soft shadow,
Her fine hair, so dark and long with a silky burnish
All dusky red with light thrown back from the burning sky.
Fiery sparks shot over us on the warm wind
And the air rippled with satanic heat.

My heart beat frantically,
Drumming like the hooves of a terrified stallion
Deep within my breast.
My throat felt dry;
My body crept with awe and tingling fear,
The door burst open; time to taste the honey.
I'd watched so many die already,
Horrified, helpless, despairing:
Now it was my turn . . .
To blend my living flesh
With glowing molten stone.

Almeena Ahmed (14)
Reath, Cardiff

The rose

Fancy lady, swathed in
Diaphanous petticoats
Attired to perfection in
Smooth silk of delicate hue.
Under the folds of her
Billowing skirts
An indiscreet, husky sweet
Perfume lures on the humming bee.
The garden's Delilah,
The eye's delight
Maturing coyly from her
Dowdy bud.
Smiling disarmingly, her
Petals unfurled
All too readily she set her
Cap at the world.

Simpering, the floral
Coquette gives her gilt-edged
Attentions to the clouds
Holding her heavy head high
Seizing all admiration
Vain as she is, she believes
Her beauty invincible
More potent than that of other flowers.
These sit beneath her
Placidly smug

As patiently they watch her,
The fragrant flirt,
For the wise plants know that
All too soon the edges of her
Petals will brown and curl
Her lovely head will droop
And shed her glory.
Her empty attributes.
They know she will die, soon,
Leaving a pile of wrinkled
Debris and nothing else.
For, behind the beauty
And the charm
Within the deepest folds of
Sun-drenched pink silk
There is nothing.

Samantha Perry (16)
Queenswood School
Brookmans Park, Hatfield
(Age Category Winner)

The strange fruit

Weird, rattling, heavy fruit,
Hard brittle leaves
Carved on the top.
And on the bottom
A flat squashed flower,
Coloured like the Earth,
Brown, green, yellow and red.
What is hiding beneath this shell?
Perhaps it is pink,
Or yellow like the sun.
Hard as a rock,
Or squishy like jelly.
Cut the fruit in half,
And the puzzle is solved.
Mushy, white flesh,
Like an eyeball
Rolling about.
Taste it . . .
It's like sugar
Sickly sweet,
Not a fruit
I like to eat.

Melanie Horne (7)
Neston C.P. School
Corsham, Wilts
(Age Category Winnr)

Vase of flowers

Vase, vase
Vase of flowers
You will soon wilt and die
But
Never, never
Never mind.

Claire Louise Broadhurst (6)
Groby, Leicester

I hate hurricanes

I hate hurricanes,
They crash and they bash,
Horrible huge monsters.
Screaming,
Screeching,
Shrieking.
Hurricanes throw the waves,
To their sides.
Huge waves,
They smash ships and tankers.
Hurricanes rampage,
Through the waters.
Hurricanes are fearless,
And evil.
The hurricane,
Has no mercy,
It just wants to,
D E S T R O Y ! ! !

Kirsty Cook (10)
Olnafirth Primary School
Shetland

TIME, THE EVER SPINNING WHEEL

Poems about times and seasons

Summer days

Sun's hot
Feet are blazing,
Shoes are sticking
Feel like lazing.

Faces sweating
Hot all round
Cool drinks
There I found.

In the garden
People sitting
Kids running
Grans knitting.

Summer days
Are really nice
Hot days —
Bring some ice.

Bital Patel (13)
Edmonton Lower School
Edmonton, London

Summer fields

The purest of all prussian blues
amidst the corn of desert hues,
and all the wildest sunset reds
are there in the dancing poppy heads.

Seas of glittering bronze and gold
are riches beyond the merchants' hold,
whilst rubies and sapphires flame the skies
all to vanish as the summer dies.

Beth Short (16)
Taunton, Somerset

Autumn is...

Autumn is a decorator.
Stripping leaves off the trees,
scattering them to the ground,
making it look pretty.

Painting the fields brown and gold,
to get a pleasing effect.
Placing food here and there,
to satisfy everyone's tastes.

Embedding hedgehogs in holes,
to fill up the spare gaps.
Making birds fly away,
to leave everything tidy.

Why does he do it?
Why, oh why?
Because Winter is coming to visit.
Autumn wants to make a good impression.

Ilona Stretch (11)
Stowmarket Middle School
Stowmarket, Suffolk

The winter accident

Boy joyriding in stolen car.
Police car — sound of siren in boy's ears.
Ice and snow making road slippery.
Putting the brakes on,

CRASH BOOM!

Boy didn't survive.

Mathieu Ward (10)
Cottingley Primary School
Leeds

Once upon a winter

Boots shuffling
People slipping
Scarves in use
Cold air nipping

Cars hidden
Under slush
Noses snivel
Cold cheeks blush

Heating on
Houses white
Chimneys cough
Smoke light

Bits of cloud
Drop from sky
On to the ground
And passers by

Sun comes out
Starts to rise
Spring triumphant
Winter dies

Nicola Dunkley (11)
St Nicholas School,
Harlow, Essex

Summer and Winter

Isn't summer great?
Aren't the flies that get in your drink and ice-cream
And the midges that bite at your shoulders and neck
And the burning hot sun that frizzles your back
And the bees that buzz in your ear but
"Won't — hurt — you — unless — you — hurt — them"
Just great?!

And what about winter? It's wonderful too,
With its frost-mice which nibble your fingers and toes
while you wait for the bus,
With its lazy sun that gets up late and goes to bed far too
    early,
With its angry wind's pitiless gusts.
It's a bully that makes animals hide and birds fly away,
But it's wonderful anyway, don't you agree?

Rachel Sekules (15)
Kilkeel High School
Kilkeel, Co. Durham

Nightfall

Waves of darkness
Suffocate the light of day.
The moon pulls them on,
As dogs on a leash.
And like millions of
Fireflies, stars buzz and fizz
Into action.
I watch this from my window
And slowly drift into
A dream.

David Loverock (11)
Landscove C. of E. Primary School
Newton Abbot, Devon
(Age Category Winner)
(Roald Dahl Wondercrump School Award)

Dream world

Lions growl in the jungle
Tortoises sleep in the trees
Tigers stay up late
While the birds talk to the bees.

Amy Howes (5)
Sittingbourne, Kent

Pictures of the night

Girl
Standing under a halo of safe lamplight,
Not venturing into the unknown dark
Nervously concealing your identity
Like a string of pearls
Hidden around your neck.

Boy
Aimlessly wandering among dark alleys
Beer smelling, tale swapping,
Rowdy laughter, endless boasting,
Squinting in the blurry darkness
Of your dreamlike trance.

Man
Strolling home with your lifelong companion
Secure in each other's company.
Warm friendship chases away
The creeping fingers of
The encroaching night.

Cat
Queen of the velvet night you walk
Proudly stalking among rooftops,
Disdainful of distractions
Intent on your purpose
This is your kingdom.

Sky
Like a soft indigo curtain strung
Across the horizon, star studded
Tiny points of light bravely shine
Around their princess
The cold, unforgiving moon.

Dawn
Gentle fingers of golden sunlight stretch
Over the hills, bleaching the sky
A soft tinted pink. You illuminate the world
Creatures of the night run and hide
From the revealing morning.

Rachel McClusky (14)
Glossop, Derbyshire

Tomorrow

It's been ten years or so,
Since my long grass was mown
And the thistles pulled out,
And the new, fresh seeds sown.

I was left long ago,
To the cold and the warm,
And the bright, chirping birds,
And the bees in the swarm.

But the time hasn't come,
When love shows in my roots,
And the rain falls softly,
On my shoots.

With no true today,
And no true tomorrow,
I spend all of my life,
In a blanket of sorrow.

Katy Hamilton (10)
Heathlands Preparatory School
Grantham, Lincs

Time

Time —
The ever-spinning wheel,
Drinks no water,
Eats no meal.
Will not stutter,
Never stops,
Walks through walls,
Heeds not locks.
Collects our thanks,
Takes our curses.
Empties our pockets,
Fills our purses.
Brings us death,
Gives us new life,
Gives us happiness,
Causes us strife.
Has no enemy,
Has no friend,
Brought the beginning,
Brings the end.

John Pregnall (16)
The Greensward School
Hockley, Essex
(Age Category Winner)

A GLASS OF REFLECTIONS

Poems of thought and consideration

I Know

I know what I think
But I do not
I know what I think
But I forgot!

Laura Jane Smith (4)
Newmarket, Suffolk

Where is?

Where is the short hair
I had
Before it grew?

On my head.

Where is my Grandad
Who had a heart attack
When I was small?

I think he's in heaven.

Where is the teddy
That I loved
When I was small?

Up in my attic.

Where is my cot
That I slept in
When I was one, two, three, four, five?

Up in my attic too.

Where are the plastic butterflies
Which Mummy hung on my cot
When I was small?

In a suitcase in Mummy and Daddy's room.

Katy Evans (7)
Horler's Pre-preparatory School
Comberton, Cambridge

Growing

Beneath the shadow of the diving board,
You mount the concrete monster,
Step by step.
You stare into the pit of water
And at the smallest platform,
A mere three metres high,
Your security.
Now you see it as just for children.
You must move on.
Adulthood is above
And childhood seven metres down.
Now, you're inbetween,
At the middle platform
And grip the edge with painted toes.
You look up
At the highest board.
But one stage at a time,
My little friend;
You will need all your courage
To cope with this one.

Abbi Lock (14)
Debenham High School
Stowmarket, Suffolk

What shall I say?
(When a boy asks me out)

If a boy asks me out,
What do I reply?
Yes, to please him,
But not to please me.
No, to please me,
But not to please him.
What do I reply?

If a boy asks me out,
What am I to do?
Say I'll think about it.
And think till he gives in,
And goes away?
Or say I've got one,
When I haven't?
What do I say,
WHEN A BOY ASKS ME OUT?

Vicky Hewish (13)
Blessed Edward Jones High School
Rhyl, Clwyd

Listen:

If I said to you,
"I have all the usual characteristics
Of a fellow my age",
You might call me modest.

But if I added,
"Except more so",
You might
Label me arrogant.

But if I explained,
"Those characteristics are greed and laziness",
You might condemn me for cynicism,
Generalisation,
For coming to conclusions
Without sufficient knowledge.

If I went on to say,
"I didn't really mean that",
When I saw the look in your eye,
You might think me weak,
Or a liar.

So I would hastily add,
"But people are lazy",
Then you would accuse me
Of judging others.

You would command me:
"Stop picking at the speck in your brother's eye!

Pause.

When all the time there is a plank in your own!"

But what does that make you?
And what does this poem make me?

Toby Quash (16)
Christ College
Brecon, Powys

Who am I?

I walk alone
Through streets of strangers
Their faces blur, merging into one.
I am unable to comprehend
What it all means.
My sense of isolation is overwhelming
How can it be that they know who they are
And yet I, standing still
While the everyday chaos
Moves around me,
I am no longer sure of my identity
Of my status in life.

Then a thought stirs
In the depths of my mind.
And slowly I begin to understand
Why I am the only one to see the madness,
Occurring wherever I look,
While the rest of the world rushes by.
In this sea of bodies
Only mine is real,
And the turmoil that I see
Is merely a twisted imagining
In my warped mind.

The chaos that I saw
Now takes another form
With my perception of the truth.
I marvel at the workings
Of my sadistical mind,
As I realise that I have the control,
All that I see, I want to see.
Without me, the people surrounding me
Would cease to exist.
And with this knowledge I conceive
That I'm no longer no-one,
But the only one.

Sarah Johns (17)
Crowthorne, Berks

Free?

What was the reason for my birth?
Why was I put upon this earth?
How will my life now proceed?
Am I a part of some big plan
That God now holds within his hands?
What will I grow up to be?
A doctor saving people's lives?
A jockey racing down the track?
A dancer leaping on the stage?
Or a teacher teaching little brats?
Will I have a choice to do something that is just for me
Or am I part of some big plan,
Not FREE! but held in God's great hands?

Lucy Martin (8)
St Bernard's School,
Newton Abbot, Devon

Face

My face is a
Trophy of my
Life.
The scars of Accident,
Stupidity,
Ignorance.
And Gallantry,
The beams of success,
The sunny grins of victory.
A traitor,
It reveals
Secrets.

James Brilliant (13)
King's School
Canterbury, Kent

Death

Lurking in the darkest corners,
Silently awaiting his prey,
Clad in black, face pinched and white,
Death is on his way.

Life is spreading round the bleak earth,
Taking it into its warm embrace.
Death passes by, with a frosty breeze
But Life just stares Death in the face.

There is a clash of swords as Life fights Death.
But Death won't be beaten with ease.
Life lunges at Death and he falls to the ground
And begs Life for mercy on his knees.

Kate McGeoch (11)
Lawhead Primary School
St Andrews, Fife

The city people meet themselves

The city people meet themselves
as they stare in the mirror of the opposite seat.
An old woman smiles at her reflection —
a girl, who's late for work
and urges the train on with a tapping foot —
the crumpled old woman remembers when
her feet tapped to speed up life
but now the feet are tired and old
and each step aches with dwindling hours;
a starched commuter tries not to look
at the broken-down man who cries —
his shallow eyes, pools of hopelessness,
the business man prays that life will be kind
and the treadmill of time will not leave him to cry
in the loneliness of a busy train;
an eager boy gapes at his reflection,
a huge man whose long arms reach to the straps
and smothers the boy in an aura of greatness —
the boy longs for the distant time
when his arms will reach
into the unknown realms of adulthood;

a worn out mother stares across
and sees another woman with the same gaze
grateful for child, but mournful for freedom.
Their eyes meet in silent conversation.

Rosanne Flynn (14)
North London
(Poet of the Year)

We didn't need money

We didn't need money.
You can't buy the sound of the waves.
You see dragonflies over the creeks for nothing.
You see marsh harriers floating over the marshes and don't
    pay a penny.
You can't pay for the sound of a woodpecker's cry.
There are sand martins flying to their tunnel nests,
And no-one demands an entrance fee.
You look at the sea sparkling and there's no charge.
It doesn't cost you to explore the orange and yellow cliffs.
There's no charge for standing on the beautiful clifftop,
Gazing out over the water.
Money isn't necessary.
It's all there and it's perfectly free.

Amy Battey (9)
Combs Ford C.P. School
Stowmarket, Suffolk

Just an old lady

I'm just an old lady who likes church socials and "do's",
Women's Institutes and stepping into everybody else's
  shoes,
Some people call me a busybody, an old gossip and a hag,
But I just ignore them, I care not if they rag.
I run the Knitting Circle, I'm a Sunday School teacher as
  well,
Oh, I drum into the children what their parents never tell,
I run the baking stall at the church's Summer Fair,
And I never miss the School Open Day — if I do, that's very
  rare.
I'm the backbone of the community, if you see what I mean
I make sure people have manners and are well and truly
  clean.
If there is a crime, the criminal I'll dig out and search,
And oh *how* I condemn those sinners who never visit
  church.
I am the speaker at the debate, I am the judge of the flower
  show
I am the opener of fairs, I am the race starter who says
  "Go!"
Nothing is complete without me being there,
No social, no institute, no local Summer Fair.
My opinions of people are truthful and are candid,
I manage to run my village entirely single-handed.

Jessica Childs (11)
Bolton, Lancs

Wishes

I sometimes wish
That life was a dream,
That friends were honest
And were how they seemed.
That parents understood
And weren't so stern,
That when the truth was told,
The truth wouldn't burn.
That when a secret was told
That secret was kept,
That when I spent money,
There would be no debt.
That people could be trusted
And just wouldn't lie,
That the ones I love
Wouldn't have to say goodbye.
That when I was hurt
I wouldn't need to cry
But most of all
We wouldn't have to die.

Marie Curran (14)
James Allen Girls School
East Dulwich, London

The mirror on life

I am a glass of reflections,
Of exactness.
Though I change left to right,
I do not change sorrow into happiness.
I gaze into the world,
Seeking truth.
People look into my eye and see reality
Of despair, happiness or madness.

My rectangular form is my outer layer,
Yet my truthful inner layer is of darkness
Until darkness is shattered by lights and faces
Of a boy who lives in my accommodation.
He is unhappy, and sick.
I watch him every day
Until at the end of time he passes away.
I was his mirror on life.

Nicholas Tyabji (10)
University College School
Hampstead, London

SUCH A PAIN

Poems of private sadness
or complaint

Now!! YES!!! No!!

A kid's life

L.A.U.R.A.A.A.A.A.A.!
Get upstairs and tidy your room NOW!
Don't do that,
Leave him alone,
Stop picking your nose,
Clean your teeth,
How dare you,
Eat your dinner,
Do your homework,
Go to bed,
Get up,
Get off that computer NOW!
Hurry up,
Switch the telly off,
Lay the table,
Wash up,
Make your bed,
Feed the rabbits,
Don't be stupid,
Don't be rude,

Naughty girl,
Don't fluffle the dogs at the table,
NO!
YES!
I DON'T KNOW!
DON'T ASK ME!
Go away!
Bring your washing down,
Come on,
Don't be such a pain,
Go and give this to the goat,
Why are you always so difficult?

Laura Maskell (11)
Dame Janet Junior School
Ramsgate, Kent

Empty schoolyard

The last person leaves,
Rushing from the end of another school day,
Leaving the playground empty,
Apart from me.

I start to walk,
Through the now-dark shelter,
Where in the day schoolbags lie,
And people climb the wooden struts on the wall.

I make my way up the playground,
Past the concrete lines,
Where in the day people run up and down,
Pretending to be aeroplanes.

I walk past the white wall,
With muddy marks that hang like clouds,
Where in the day footballs thud their tune,
And people cry out the score.

I jog past the furrow in the grass,
A scar on green skin,
Where in the day people skid,
Shouting and laughing.

And then *I* start to run,
Putting *my* jacket in the shelter *I* climb the wooden struts
on the wall.
Then *I* run down the concrete lines,
Pretending to be an aeroplane.

I kick *my* muddy football against the white wall,
Skid down the grass . . .

And wait for tomorrow.

Calum Brown (11)
Foyers Primary School
Foyers, By Inverness
(Age Category Winner)

Moaning

I don't like spiders, (they don't like me)
I don't like people who dunk biscuits in tea,
I hate being left just hanging on phones
I don't like the dark, or red traffic cones,
The sight of blood just makes me go pale,
And 'in date bread' that's patently stale!

I can't abide motorists 'kangarooing' at lights,
Or BHS with their itchy blue tights,
Smug vegetarians with loony food fads,
Mobile phones and Radion ads,
I've never liked milk from the day I was born,
Or that 'Jolly Green Giant' on the tins of sweetcorn.

Those gruesome TV shows that ask you to ring
And vote for some moron that never could sing,
Or Slimfast promotions for milkshakes in pink,
With terrible actors whose lips aren't in sync,
And my dog who comes panting, and all out of breath,
After trying to bark a small hedgehog to death.

And American Evangelists who knock on our door,
Getting rid of these people is just such a chore,
I listen intently and give them a nod,
Then tell them our neighbour is searching for God!

I can't stomach peppers, I can't abide parties,
I've never liked nuts and I've never liked Smarties,
I don't like wasps and I don't like bees,
And I can't stand cauliflower covered in cheese,
And I can't abide people who talk through their hat,
They moan about this and they moan about that,
Hold on a minute, what's this I see,
These sort of people sound rather like me!

Lisa Story (15)
James Allen Girls School
East Dulwich, London

National finals

The time draws close,
Only a night away, before
I must compete.
How I dread it.
How I anticipate it.
Shall it go well.
Shall it not.

The time is now.
The lights, sound, people I must ignore.
Concentrate.
Remember.
Concentrate.
On the routines.
I do.

All over now.
And yet
The excitement is still there.
The adrenalin still pumps
Throughout.
The mistakes, and
The excelling.
All over now.

A year ago.
The memories are confused.

What went wrong then.
I know not.
It matters not.
It's over, finished.
Unless I compete again.

Stephen Whitney (15)
Thorpe St Andrew School
Norwich
(School of the Year)

Words

Words uttered orally fall
Flat and dead,
Struck down by the inhibitions
In my head,
And my tongue, forever tied,
Forever slow, betrays me.

Ink and paper serve me better,
Faithful friends with every letter.
Never betraying me as I write,
Naked and dark.

Paul Garrad (16)
Billericay, Essex

"Next please!"

I entered the cold atmosphere of a white room,
Gave my name, stumbled towards a chair, and joined
the row of others.
People cower beneath posters with smiling faces.
I look around in a feeble attempt to escape.
I'm enclosed by four walls
decorated with all I hate in the world —
Paperwork and Pain
operating as a partnership.
Inmates of the waiting room shudder with the drill
Until a victim is finally released
Greeted by sympathetic faces.
Still numbed by the experience, she is presented
with a sticker —
Her only reward.
The Dentist's surgery — a white room, surrounded by
white faces bearing white teeth
ruled by the expertise of White Coats.
A Clinical Clearing —
Where adults become victims of childhood fears.

Karen McGavock (17)
Webster's High School
Angus, Scotland

Migraine attack

As I waken, I feel strange.
I can't think right or remember anything.
What day is it? Where am I? Who am I?
There is a deep banging from the centre of my brain
As if someone is hitting
Hitting
Hitting
Me with a hammer.
I look around.
Everything seems fuzzy and blurred.
I see some light.
It feels like someone cracking
Smashing
Breaking
My head with a pneumatic drill.
The excruciating pain grows greater and greater
Until I feel that I can take no more.
Why does it have to be so sore?
I hear a noise, it is so loud, magnified by the pain!
It was a voice that I heard.
It sounds muffled, deafeningly loud.
I try to shout, "Go away," but it doesn't seem to come out
    right.
I feel really confused.
The banging continues.
I try to lift my arm, but it is lifeless.
Dead,

Uncontrollable.
It won't move.
I start to retch,
My body wants to be sick,
But my stomach is empty,
Heaving uselessly.
I want to die!
A handful of pills are thrown down my throat.
After a while, I start to feel better.
Eventually, I am back to normal . . .
Until the next attack.
Why me? Why me?

Andrew Turner (14)
Kilkeel High School
Kilkeel, County Down

Operation

I am wheeled through buzzing corridors.
I watch the moving ceiling
until my heavy eyes submit to sleep.

Confused, in a blur of light,
mysterious faces slide in silhouette.
Struggling from the chains of sleep —
each link pulling me down —

I try to steady the faces.
I speak,
but only a croak reaches the surface
of my submersion in myself.

They aim their discussion at me
and gather round to stare.
"Her eyes look almost open,
do you think she can hear?"

I answer inside,
tearing at my solid bonds
until my whole body shakes.
The shady figures do not hear me;
they cannot feel my silent cry.
A disjointed hand
strokes my forehead tenderly.
The warm touch melts an iron link
and one by one the others fall away.

Rosanne Flynn (14)
North London
(Poet of the Year)

The visit

There was the smell of cleanness
As we walked through the corridor,
We had gone to visit my great-grandad
And I still remember the frail man
Who sat in the claws of an armchair.
His eyes were seeping with moist tiredness.
He beckoned to me,
"Come and sit on my lap."
Not known for my shyness,
I bounded as a frog would onto a lily pad.
He was as breakable
As a pencil lead.
But he smiled,
As I gave him the hot, sticky
Box of Roses . . .
And I saw his teeth, pale brown swimmers
In a sea of white spit.
His long bony hand trembled
As he tried to open the box.
But a starchy soldier nurse
Came and plucked me off his lap.

She placed his dinner on the table.
A dog's dinner
of peas, carrots, potato and gravy,
All splashed into a silver bowl made out of foil.
He picked up the plastic spoon
And offered it to me.
But I shook my head
And reached for the Roses.

Elizabeth Ann Wilcock (13)
Halesworth Middle School
Halesworth, Suffolk

My Granddad lives by candlelight

Geoffrey is my Granddad.
He's spirited, stubborn, stately, eighty
And dying.

You see,
My Granddad lives by candlelight.
Fearing the playful shadows of darkness —
Of the absence of light.
The shadows of death,
That Dance around him.

He sits at the supper table,
Dribbling gravy down his front.
He's saying how he met his wife —
"Falling in love in the fall of 'forty two'."
He grins with sly wit
He breaks out into a wartime song,
A serenade he used to sing for her.
And he starts to cough
Violently.
The shadows jump.
Death has breathed on the flame.
But he's saying it
Because he will never be able to say it again,
For his candle is burning low,
And he knows it.

Occasionally the wick grows small.
The wax begins to harden,
The arteries grow thinner,
The heart pumps slower.
Quickly the wax is poured out,
The blood is changed in his body,
The light grows again —
Slowly, falteringly.
Never to be as bright as before.

"Let's go for a walk, on the Downs," he says.
Smiling, nostalgically.
An uneasy silence descends.
We can see his shadow

Flickering in front of us.
"You'll have to keep warm," says his wife.
Nervously.
We drive up there anyway —
To where he used to walk for days on end.
"Geoffrey Stallibrass – PRESIDENT of the SUSSEX
    DOWNSMEN."
"I hope I'm not slowing you down," he whispers.
It's cold and windy,
The flame flickers.
"Not at all," I lie,
Walking pigeon step next to him.
We talk.
We walk, maybe 100 metres.
Maybe less.
We walk back now,
Slower.
 His wife puts her arm around his shoulder,
Supporting him.
My Granddad's spirited, stubborn, stately, and eighty,
But a deformed, forlorn, cripple totters back.
Silent.
Sad.
Next time he'll walk 50 metres,
Maybe less,
And he knows it.
Because his flame is spluttering,
Being gutted by the congealing wax,
 The residue of a once fierce fire.
Yes, he knows it,

He knows it all too well,
For Geoffrey will die by candlelight.

David Thake Stallibrass (14)
Hampstead School
London
(Age Category Winner)

Angry

I shout,
I stamp,
I bounce around,
I stamp up the stairs,
I bounce on my bed,
Then my sister tries to calm me back down
So then I go outside where the trees are rattling
Then I feel it is a world of badness.
Then I go in the house and say I am sorry.

Donna Fisher (7)
Whitehall Infants School
Walsall

Father – a name given to God

You've reduced me to humiliation again,
Slow torture,
Each word you utter scrapes against my eardrums
as sandpaper to an open wound,
In this bid to demand my respect you twist
the knife a little more,
Just a little more,
The bile, the vomit and the abhorrence well up from
    inside,
I'm retching now,
I can taste it,
Taste the bitter slime of your words in my mouth,
Seeping between my teeth,
Sliding down my gums
and stagnating in my heart,
My silence infuriates you,
So you stab me again and again,
Stuck all over with pins
Like a voodoo doll,
I drag my waxen body away,
Away from your contemptuous eyes as blood pours
like tears from my wounds.

Kerry Capiron (17)
Francis Bacon School
St Albans, Herts

Masks

A mask is . . .
a thing that covers our feelings
and makes us someone we're not.
It helps us disguise our emotions
like an undercover detective.

We wear a mask when . . .
we're hurt
and we don't want to show
how we feel.

I wear a mask when
I am sad,
jealous
or tense
and don't want people seeing how
sad I am.

I wear a mask when . . .
My mum is telling me off for things
I wish I hadn't done.

Sometimes my mask is not good enough
and friends see through.

Sometimes I feel like telling someone
But I am afraid.

Ayse Turgut (11)
Wembley Manor Junior School
Wembley, Middlesex

Outbreak

My sorrow clamours for release,
A wild horse, confined.
A horse that would gallop far, far away
Hooves fleeting over rocks and stones.

What could prevent
The powerful muscles striving
For freedom.
Plunging deep into wild country
Where man can never set foot.

The cool, refreshing air
Breathed deep into the lungs.
The wind tugging at the wild mane,
Lashing at the face.
Blood pounding, the invincible excitement of freedom
Spurs the wild horse
To run from everything
And everyone.

116   WONDERCRUMP POETRY!

Then, growing tired, the horse slows,
A wonderful sense of loneliness descends,
The only sounds are the wind
And silence.
Silence, a deafening roar, overpowering.

The sun is setting.
The beautiful gold and red glow
Cast over the world.
The dark coat of the beast
Bathed with vivid colour
The horse is free,
Alone.

Rain begins to fall
Prancing, the horse welcomes the rain
Cool rivulets mingle red with gold.

By a pool the animal bows its head
And drinks.
The rain is torrential.
The sun has retired.
In its place the moon shines steadily
Reflecting the mellow light
Into the mind,
Calming.
But happiness remains
In new freedom.

Amelia Jane Wilkinson (17)
Forest Hill, London

Bedtime

Tiredness is like a cold
It catches you sooner or later.
When it does you find
Your eyes can't take the strain.
Slowly you drift away until
Finally you switch off, only
Your heart is still working.

Luke Thomson (11)
Brightlands School
Glos

ZZzz

Trust

When I had that trust,
I never realised what it gave me
It was only when I lost it that
I knew it couldn't save me

One false move and it's gone
And you know you can't regain
The way it was before
You caused them so much pain

Now I have to work
To find my piece of mind
I'll always have the task
Of earning back what once was mine.

Isobel Hinings (16)
Thorpe St Andrew School
Norwich
(Age Category Winner)
(School of the Year)

Moving house

It seems strange.
The bare walls,
The empty mantelpiece,
The carpet marked with rings
remembering where the sofa stood.
A forgotten book.
A spotlight of sun on the stair
where our cat Pickles slept.
My footsteps echo now on floorboards,
Soon new people will come
and break our souls as they
cut lino and chip paint.

Lauren Coffey (9)
Handford Hall Primary School
Ipswich

THE SUN BEGAN TO FADE

Poems of public protest

At the edge

I met a dying soldier
At the edge of a river of blood.
He had fought to help other people,
Yet they left him to die in the mud.

I met a crying mother
At the edge of a river of tears.
She now realised war wasn't romantic,
And she hurt for her son's wasted years.

I met a jobless father
On top of a mountain of debt.
Christmas was just round the corner,
There was so much his kids wouldn't get.

I met a worried miner
On the side of a cliff of dismay.
His foothold was one man's decision;
He was praying it wouldn't give way.

I met an innocent school-girl
At the start of the roadway of life.
She was frightened of what was before her,
She saw fighting and crying and strife.

She saw flowers that were poisoned and wilting,
Bare plains where forests once stood.

Animals dying, or losing their homes;
Nobody helping as much as they could.

There were coils of nasty barbed-wire
On top of graffitied stone walls.
Lorries and diggers and shouting
Were drowning out the birds' calls.

She saw fairytales ending in nightmares.
She was angry at what she could see.
And when I looked at her closely
I realised that this girl was me.

Julie Duffin (14)
Coleraine High School
Coleraine, N. Ireland

ist

Belligerent human
(If *human* is right)
Employs difference
As his form of spite.

I described 'him' as male,
Perhaps this is confusing,
Maybe 'it' is the pronoun
Which I should be using.

Sexist, racist and
Homophobic is he.
The outside of people
Is all he can see.

Obsolete is equality
In this man's eyes,
Anyone different
He will despise.

Be it sex or religion
Or colour of skin,
He's there with his insults,
Both shallow and thin.

But of all disabilities,
His is the main.

For although being human,
He isn't humane.

Toby Rome (14)
Worthing High School
Worthing, West Sussex

Last thoughts of a convicted murderer

In Missouri, people found guilty of murder are executed by three lethal injections. This man has been convicted of murder; for six months he has been imprisoned and taught how to die. Now he is in the execution chamber, seeing his family for the last time . . . upside down. He is waiting for the three injections to wipe him out. These are his last thoughts.

I'm innocent, proven guilty.
What life I have
Is upside down;
My last view, the wrong way round.
Six months, I have been trained to die;
Taught How? Where? When?
And Why?
Now the time has come,
I don't believe.
. . . Never wrong,

But no reprieve.
Confined into my silent world.
My friends, family and
Loved ones; heard
Me scream inside.
Nothing could they do,
But cry . . .
Only three injections to wipe out the world,
I'm innocent
But no-one heard.

Alexandra Sarah Champion (14)
Ulverston, Cumbria

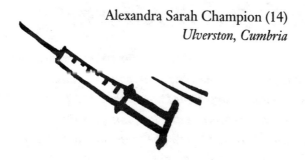

No-one cared

Pretty girl,
sitting there,
Beaten and bruised.
No-one cared.

Pretty girl,
on her own,
Confidence lost.
All alone.

Pretty girl,
hurt too much,
Lost her loving.
Scared to touch.

Pretty girl,
lost and cold,
lost her feelings.
Rape untold.

Pretty girl,
hurt too long,
lost her freedom.
Lost and gone.

Sophie O'Callaghan (15)
Bruton, Somerset

The saviour's welcome

I can just imagine the headline:
"The Almighty: truth or myth?"
Unshaven reporters
Sip mineral waters
Press conferences commence . . .

"Now, Mr Christ, please tell me truly:
Are you really the Son of God?"
"Smile for Camera 1."
Bedlam's begun,
Morning News, please copy.

It's hit the radio: "Into the Night —
The Exclusive with Jesus Christ."
The "Miracle Man"
The "Master Plan"
"Mankind, hear good news!"

The television is next on the agenda -
"Wear Nike Airs! Jesus Christ does."
The "Public's friend"
(Where does it end?)
The Face that launched an Ad-Campaign.

Interviews all over the world
An international buzz
They seek Him here

They seek Him there
But where He is, it seems He was . . .

A Number 1 hit for the Ultimate Redeemer
A cover of an old favourite
The grannies smile
The "Jesus File"
A kind of "New Age" Proclaimer

Not revered as the Holy Lamb of God,
Not blessed by all mankind
The Sovereign Lord,
The one Adored (?)
Is exploited — typical.

Jill Reynolds (15)
Preston Comprehensive School
Yeovil, Somerset

Special ABC

Adapting to my company
Boisterous, fun and forceful. Yet
Considered strange. They are unlike us,
Disabled.
Experience is the word.
Future? What does it hold for them?

Gladly pulling you by the
Hand. Showing you their school.
Impatient, and no signs of shyness.
Joyful at this brand new visitor. Me.
Kindly teachers tend their every need
Loving and so friendly, learning how to cope,
Meeting difficulties the rest of us will not.
Noticing not our differences. Yet,
Others do.
Prejudged by society,
Quick to judge, slow to
Respond to the
Special Needs.
'The Unit'. Place of tears, learning and fun.
U is for the understanding needed, but by many, not
shown.
Vulnerable.
Wheelchairs, crutches, heavy pushchairs fill the corridor
Experience is the word.
Young and unaware of problems to come. Their
Zeal for life is apparent.

Rachel Owen (17)
Brynteg Comprehensive School
Bridgend, Mid Glamorgan

Emily

Head down she shuffles along
Old, uncared for, her care-worn cheeks are streaked with
  tears.
Husband dead, her family don't want to know.
Her grandchildren have been told she's dead.
Told she passed away peacefully in her sleep.
All she has left is her clothes and a bag full of cups and
  saucers.
They were given to her by her mother.
They are in pieces now, but still she pulls them along.
She has her memories, lots of memories.
She walks around, reliving the good times.
Eternally chatting to the same neighbour about the same
  thing.
Oh, hello! How's George? Your cat's looking very healthy!
Just make sure it keeps off my petunia bed!
This she endlessly chants, endlessly shutting out her
  appalling reality.
She'll die some day, but no one will know.
Or care.
Oh, hello! How's George? Your cat's looking very healthy!
Just make sure it keeps off my petunia bed!

David Tulley (12)
Stewartfield, East Kilbride
(Age Category Winner)

Warrington bomb

Two tiny boys, small children playing.
Looking for a card, mother's day soon.
Red rubbish bin silently ticking.
Having trouble parking, can't find a space.
"Meet you at McDonalds, I'll park the car."
Children running past the red rubbish bin.
Big Bang. Time stood still.
People running, people screaming.
Two tiny boys, small limbs bleeding.
Somewhere in Ireland, people are smiling.
Somewhere in England, people are crying.

Rosie Clarke (14)
Sir William Robertson High School
Welbourn, Lincoln
(Age Category Winner)

God's baby, man's mistake

He's a small human being,
Who lies on a bed
With little strength left,
But he still rocks his head.
He lies there alone,
With despair in his eyes
He's too weak to protest.
You won't hear his cries.
His mother has left him,
He's now on his own.
A filth-ridden mattress
Is this baby's home.
He needs a cuddle
And someone to hold,
To care for and love him
And shut out the cold.
He lives in a world,
Where hopefulness fades,
A Romanian baby
Dying of AIDS.

> Katie Miller (14)
> *Rudheath High School*
> *Rudheath, Cheshire*

Yesterday's day

Crime, secrecy and fear
Filled the Warsaw sky
Pain, terror and dread
Stopped at every house
And banged with the fist of reality
On the window
Knocking violently on every door,
There was no escape.

At one house
The swirling blackness of life
Stopped at the gate.
It could go no further.
For in the window stood a Chanukivan.
Nine tiny flames:
Each a shield against evil.
Each a single sword fighting for good.
The city sky breathed deeply and
A huge swell of energy
Roared along the rooftops, urging branches to stop,
To listen.
The sky was remembering the pain of yesterday.

A time when a Chanukivan in the window
Meant certain death
For its owner.
A time when there were no thoughts or ideas.
No plans. No adventures.
A time when the might of a single man
Had silenced a town.
A fearful hush had washed over Warsaw
And hung all opinions out to dry.
The city sighed.
It was remembering mass censorship of minds.
All children listening to
A new kind of teacher.
All parents afraid:
Lowering their heads in silent obedience.
Shame and defeat.
An uneasy restlessness patrolled the streets.
The shadow of a new kind of guard.
Along a station's windswept platform.
A soldier, as he walked, was remembering:

> *"The mightiest enemy of the Aryan is the Jew . . .*
> *. . . He is always a parasite"*

The words of his leader echoed
In his head, synchronized with the
Clicking of his boots on the concrete platform.
There, lying at his feet, was a
Jewish lawyer.
He had only one eye,

one hand,
one foot.
The partner to each had been torn off
By the sharp sword of anti-semitism.
Part of his skull was missing,
It had been replaced by a silver plate.

As he looked at the dying man
The soldier showed no emotion.
No grief. No compassion.
He remembered only the lies he had been taught,
The lies which stripped him of feelings.

The roar of the train signalled
Its departure.
The guard stepped back.
From the carriage rows of
Little children stared down with
Sad, confused eyes.
"Why won't this man help us?" they sobbed.
The soldier saw none of this.
He looked straight past the children and
Ignored the future, as the train slowly rolled away.
The children stared back through haunting eyes.
They were going to a camp,
But it was certainly no holiday.

In the station
The man on the platform lay dying,
Alone and helpless

In the fading light.
The yellow from the Star of David
Embedded into his clothing
Shone out boldly into the darkness.

The city sky choked back its tears.
No crime of today, no unspoken fear of modern life
Could ever equal the horror of the past.
And the sky looked through the window of the house,
Looked at the family celebrating Chanukah.
At that second, the future saw the past.
The city stepped back in time
Frozen, motionless.
And then, sobbing to itself, it turned
And glided down the street.

But as it turned the corner, it knew
It was too late.
Even the children of today, too young to remember,
Would never forget the horror of
The Nazi Holocaust.
The pain and fear that had burned in the
Heart of every Jew.
The sickening, pointless waste of life.
The city was crying uncontrollably now.
For it had seen, as it looked in the window of the house,
The sadness of the past.
On the arm of the grandfather were
Two numbers.
Means of identification

He would never be allowed to forget.
Burnt into his arm was an unwanted reminder.

A permanent tattoo of time.

Anna Lewis (16)
Brynteg Comprehensive School
Bridgend, Mid Glamorgan

A soldier's fears

A soldier fears
For his life
As he runs
Through the streets

A soldier fears
For his life
As he guards
The towns and streets

A soldier feared
For his life.
But he died.
He got shot.

A soldier's wife,
feared for his life.

She doesn't have to
worry now . . .

Does she?

Sara Ainley (12)
Sheldon, Birmingham
(Age Category Winner)

It's not my fault

It's not my fault, I didn't do
anything, why should *I* do anything
    It's not *my* fault
I'm not firing harpoons into
whales or shooting elephants.
    It's not *my* fault
How can *I* stop all this happening
and anyway, there's plenty more
fish in the sea (isn't there?)

Michael Shephard (10)
St Catherine's R.C. Primary School
Littlehampton, West Sussex

Victim of war

Terrified,
The little boy crouches
In a corner of the aid centre.
Around him
Nurses whizz by,
Bright lights flash.
There is a strong smell of disinfectant.
The floor, hard and shiny,
Seems to spin.
He huddles into his grey rags
For comfort.
Where is he?
He does not remember much.
He remembers his mother
As he has last seen her.
Laughing.
Whirling in light.
She was not on the train
To the aid centre.
Where is she now?
Is she still in Bosnia?
There was a man
On the train
Who took the boy on his knee
And told him
Not to be afraid.
Was that his father?

He does not know.
His past his present his future
Grey mist.
What will happen to him?

Maggie Von Kaenel (10)
Charlbury School
Charlbury, Oxon
(Age Category Winner)

Peace not war

Stop this war,
End the crime,
It's gone too far,
Now is the time.
Lay down your gun,
Let's all unite,
Bring on the fun,
We reject the fight.

Towns in ruin,
People dead,
Families broken,
Gone the head.
Children in tears,
Mothers cry,

Coffins are lowered,
Too many die.

Now's the time,
Show your face,
You're not part,
Of the human race.
God made us all,
To work and love,
Hide the masks,
Produce the dove.

Stephen Kearney (10)
St Patrick's Primary School
Dunnamanagh, Strabane
(Age Category Winner)

A few drops of rain

A few drops of rain,
Fell on some grain,
But not enough.

A family were given wheat,
For them to eat,
But not enough.

A little girl starved,
The village cared,
But not enough.

Few mourned,
Some worked,
But not enough.

The chief was angry,
He tried to be kind,
But not hard enough.

The village split,
Fought against each other,
As if that wasn't enough.

The country split,
Took sides with the village,
If that was not enough.

The world joined in,
World War Three broke out,
The earth had enough!

The sky turned grey,
The sun began to fade.
And all for the want of a few drops of rain

Katherine Fields (12)
West Wycombe C.C. School
West Wycombe, Bucks

The cattle mart

Frightened inside a stuffy lorry
Nothing but blackness to see
Shut out from the outside world
Crushed and cramped.

People selling and buying cows
Standing round a dusty ring
Looking like patient cats sitting, waiting
Round a cage of gerbils.

Everyone wearing green or brown
Like newts resting in red-brown pond mud
The shaken cow seems nervous
As people crowd round.

Men with long sticks
Force the cow to walk
Round and round
Just for all to see.

The cracking sticks
On the cow's back
Sound like popcorn
Being dropped slowly into a pan.

Curiously sniffing the people
It paws the cold hard wall
Like a spider trying in vain
To climb out of a glass jar.

A musty smell drifts with a tint of dung
Metal gates open and close
Like the inside of a prison
With people rattling the doors
Trying to get free.

The cow moans
As if in pain
There isn't much else to see
Except cruelty.

Elaine Wilson (11)
Moy Primary School
Moy, Inverness-shire

Trapped in the zoo

Freedom lost
Joy gone
why should I
carry on?

Horrid food
no sun
nothing new
no fun.

People point
People stare
children laugh —
they don't care.

Cold and wet
day and night
Pride broken —
no fight.

Some are old,
weak and frail
Zoos aren't homes
They're **JAIL**

Anna Goodman (11)
James Allen Preparatory School
East Dulwich, London

People paid for this

The bull waited in the cramped pen
The bars pressing him down
Outside the humans thirst for blood
People paid for this.

He's crazed by meat
His own dead brother
He knows not what is about to happen
People paid for this.

The bars fly up
He's made to go out
Out to face his own death
People paid for this.

The Picador raced towards him
Making him toss the padded white horse
The first stage in a slow death
People paid for this.

Once he is weak the death man comes
Stabbing him to die
He falls exhausted, death screams
People paid for this.

All that is left is a pool of blood
And some ears in an envelope
A pointless sacrifice.

People paid for this.

Katherine Forster (10)
St Catherine's R.C. Primary School
Littlehampton, West Sussex
(Age Category Winner)

Harpoon

Now near extinction,
The fate of the whale is sealed,
By a shaft of steel.

I wrote this poem to put emphasis onto the hellish life of the hunted whales. Every year hundreds of whales are slaughtered, and if this continues, there will be none left.

Daniel Smith (15)
Smestow School
Wolverhampton

The walk

Yesterday
Our class visited the sea-shore
To search for sea creatures
And a whole lot more
But all we found were

Plastic toys, teddies and cubes
Tin cans, squashed and empty
Crisp paper bags and bottle tops
Polystyrene that will never rot
All this in one afternoon
On the sea-shore
A whole lot of pollution
And not much more

Michelle Walker (7)
Saltburn Primary School
Saltburn, Cleveland
(Age Category Winner)

Lethal cargo

A tanker of greed —
Money and oil —
Cheap crews —
A breeze —
A gale —
A horrific wind —
A coffin ship —
Nature's weather —
Man is powerless —
Engines stop —
Splutter and sput —
Drifting helplessly —
Bang!
Oil pours —
Spews and coughs —
Birds die —
Salmon suffer —
Seals lie gasping —
It's destroying —
Killing —
Poisoning —
All because of us —
Our avaricious want for oil.

Hayley Elizabeth Duncan (11)
Olnafirth Primary School
Voe, Shetland

WHO WILL GO FIRST?

Poems of the animal world

The dolphin

Who knows what untold mysteries
Lie dormant in your mind,
The liquid of your movements,
The kindness of your kind?

Your sleekly-patterned dorsal fin
Slides silent through the sea;
Who can see the truth of you,
The truth of you, or me?

Your high-pitched chattering is loud,
As you plunge into the deeps,
Your body's active, very sure,
While your mind as surely sleeps.

The shadows glide upon the rocks
As you flex overhead
To conjure food between the cracks
Of the sea's silver bed.

The mildness of your works of art,
Is sculptured in your grin,
The only smile that's wider
Is the one that lives within.

Water-colour creature
That neither runs nor fades,

The paper that you're painted on
Is water-marked with waves.

The people come, the dolphins come,
Not only for the fish,
But also for the company,
The dolphin's human wish.

A truly independent hound,
You follow ships, you follow boats,
With very few necessities,
But many, many hopes.

Daniel Parmenter (12)
University College School
Hampstead, London

Seal

The rocks
Jut out of the water,
Like sea serpents.
He looks like a slug
Sitting on the serpent's head.

He pushes himself off the rock . . .
His head is like a skull,

Bobbing in the sea.
His body is made of soft black clay.
A knife chiselled the grooves,
Carefully,
In his fan-like tail.
His nose, a scrap of plastic,
 Painted with Humbrol Black Enamel Paint.
His whiskers, nylon thread,
Poke through his soft clay head.
His eyes, varnished pebbles.
His ears, playmobile wheels,
Dropped in glue, lost on the floor,
To find cat and dog hairs.
But as the moon shines,
He flicks silver pellets on the waves . . .
And he flies underwater with wings of iron.

Phoebe Josephine Wingate
Halesworth Middle School
Halesworth, Suffolk

Swallow

It is winter
again and I have
to make that big
journey back
to Africa over
the sea, over the
Sahara Desert.
Past the English
Channel, France and
Spain. It takes
me six weeks.
I do not know
how I will
stay alive.
There are
lots of
dangers like
the sand storms.
It was better
being a baby because
I did not have to do
this long journey.

Rebecca Dougall (7)
St Catherine's School
Camberley, Surrey

Barn owl

She controls the elements,
The can-can dancer who shows her white frills
Beneath her root-like legs.
Her ears are sunken deep into her head,
Almost inaccessible.
But they pick up signals like a hidden beacon.
Her eyes are sure and steady,
Unrepentant despite her many murders.
She wavers through the dimensions,
Through the mirror warps of the universe
And patrols the forest gate
Like a palace guard.
She repels the forces of chaos which invade at night
And seeps through unpainted gaps in the forest's fabric.
Driving them back with her razor-wire beak.
Then, she rides back with her cavalry
From their hard won battle.
Animated in the moonlight,
She breaks the stardust with colossal wing beats,
Her wraith-like body gliding in and out
Of the wizened oaks . . .
Her loyal servants to the very end.

Barnaby Stuart Love (13)
Halesworth Middle School
Halesworth, Suffolk

The lone hunter

In the early hours of the morning,
A golden brown kestrel hovers
Over the moors.
Its eyes catch a movement,
A small, brown mouse.
It scuttles across the thick heather
The kestrel with its back
To the rising sun.
It descends
At rapid pace,
Talons open
Eyes sharp as knives
It sweeps across the ground
Hurtling at its prey
The kestrel
Takes the mouse by its neck
Afterwards
Nothing
Could be heard.

Nathan Townsend (11)
Middleton in Teesdale School
Co. Durham

The sculptor

He stares
At the motionless block.
Within it, he sees a creature
Entombed in darkness,
Reluctant to leave.
He clasps the chisel;
He studies the stone prison;
The sharp instrument
Pierces the surface.
He strikes again;
A segment breaks away.
With delicate strokes
He chips
At the shell case.
A curved beak
Is set free;
Two hooded eyes
Stare at their creator.
The eagle is hatching.

Kim Garrard (15)
Debenham High School
Stowmarket, Suffolk
(Age Category Winner)

The bat

The bat is made . . . maybe of ash,
Charred flaked paper,
Fragile as candle flames
As he dances on pulsating heat.
A skeletal leaf body
Jerks in the wind
On hidden strings,
Like a faulty puppet.
He's a mongrel,
With his rabbit's tulip ears,
Mouse body,
And pterodactyl wings,
A wizard's rusty mobile.
His kite frame fingers
Are the scaffolding
For leathery wings . . .
Umbrellas for the insects.
Then, he hangs like a drooping flower
In a charred chrysalis,
Rooted to the cave wall.

Clare Watkinson (12)
Halesworth Middle School
Halesworth, Suffolk

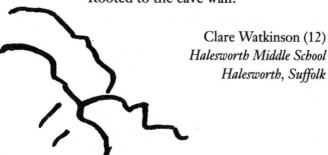

Bluebottle

Its wings beat hard.
They are built up of tiny cracks,
with blotches of colour,
like a church window.
The bluebottle is a Chippendale,
showing off its macho muscles,
blue and blotchy,
bulging out of its crumb body
like bubbles on the surface of bath water.
It buzzes over to the window,
sticks its six plungers on it
and climbs up the slippery mountain,
but with no rope.
Its eyes bulge out of their sockets
for all round vision
as it abseils down again.
It flies, circling a glass of milk,
then, landing on the rim,
brings out its long tongue,
and hoovers it up . . .
when . . .
it slips,

falling into the thick milky bog,
spinning round and round,
struggling for the side,
but not succeeding;
it floats still and stiff,
like a lost boat out at sea.

Daren John Revell (12)
Halesworth Middle School
Halesworth, Suffolk

My cat

My cat
Looks for his prey
He finds it
He stops dead still
And stalks nearer and nearer still
Then he pounces on it
Blood flows everywhere
He brings it in
A scream comes from my mother
Then dead silence.

Francesca Angelini (7)
James Allen Preparatory School
East Dulwich, London
(Age Category Winner)

Caught!

"Mouse!" you shout.
Why do you scream at me?
A harmless dusty ball of wool,
I deprive you of little
So why do you hate me?

Oh, no! Here they come
Soot-black boots —
Squeak! My poor tail!
Out he carries me.
I hang like a spider.

Ouch! I hit the path.
Wind ruffles my fur;
My whiskers tingle.
The rain falls;
I shiver and run.

The door opens;
I scamper in.
Maybe they *are* kind;
My favourite cheese!
I nibble. Snap!

Claire Chilvers (11)
Debenham High School
Stowmarket, Suffolk

Blitz cat

Surrounded by sorrow and destruction,
I walk alone.
Piles of rubble are my castles,
Pools of flame are my companions.
The UXB's, the Doodlebugs and Incendiaries,
I've surveyed them all.
What a kaleidoscope of tales I could tell.
Humans feel pain and suffering.
While I seem privileged and immune to the wasteful
violence around me.
I am a lonesome wanderer,
A black shadow,
All that's dear to me is lost, and more.
The siren goes;
The shrapnel flies;
I'm only a black cat
standing by Saint Paul's.

Kate Fellows (11)
St John's C.E. Middle School
Blakebrook, Kidderminster

The black cat

She stretches.
Her small padded paws.
Suddenly dangerous
Her claws spring out
Her small, pink mouth yawns
With dagger-sharp teeth
Like miniature stalactites
In the cavernous deep.
Her glossy coat
Shining black in the light
As she walks,
Shoulder blades moving
Her sleek fur stretching,
Seeming almost to glide,
As her body twists and turns.
Her green eyes,
With deep black pupils,
Like whirlpools
Hold me in a spell.

Jessica Meacham (11)
Brightlands School
Glos

Cheetah! Cheetah!

Cheetah, cheetah, Linford of the desert,
Devil's pussy cat,
Death at ninety miles per hour,
Killer out of nowhere!
WILDEBEEST BEWARE!

Cheetah, cheetah, fast as a bullet,
You're death on four strong legs,
Leaping, bounding, sleek as a spaniel,
Looking round for a morsel of lunch,
You are a majestic murderer!
WILDEBEEST BEWARE!

CRUNCH!

Mark Halsall (12)
Brynteg Upper Comprehensive School
Bridgend, Mid Glamorgan

Team work

Two leopards were wearing
A terrible frown.
They wriggled and jiggled
And jumped up and down.

They twisted and insisted,
"I *can* count my spots,"
Then tumbled and grumbled,
"I'm tied up in knots."

They growled and they scowled,
They hadn't a clue.
Then all of a sudden,
They knew what to do.

They bounced and announced
And shook their great paws,
"You can count my spots . . .
And I will count yours!"

Becky Collier (14)
Rudheath High School
Northwich, Cheshire

Tiger

Sleek and sly and muscular
Disguised in black and amber
Like the African grass.
The hot sun blazes on his back
Making his velvet fur shine golden.
His eyes glow as he slinks forward attentively
He prowls as if he has something
To hide
Belly down — face up,
Staring ahead.
His tail ripples,
effortlessly,
To swat the flies.
What has he seen?
What has he seen?
He licks his lips,
Jaws parted,
His teeth glitter like ivory.
Then he runs!
Faster and faster!
The antelopes see him
And huddle in a bunch.
"TIGER! TIGER!"
They seem to cry.
The lame and young ones
Hurry to the safety of the group . . .
But too late!

He selects his prey diligently
Then he pounces!
The antelope falls to the floor
And he bites into its neck.
The rest of the herd scatter
Petrified
They run for their lives . . .

But the tiger purrs contentedly . . .
He is satisfied.

Nicola Forman (10)
Melbourne Junior School
Melbourne, Derby

River bed

Gargoyle-like squats the toad,
Hideously deformed and covered in warts,
On a throne of grey rock,
Rising up from the mass of pebbles,
For an instant the water becomes
The Royal Mint, overflowing
With golden coins.
The moment gone, the river returns,
A mysterious blue, enchanting,
Deep and almost black.

A breeze ripples the pools
That are home to tiny fish
And it sounds
As if the fish themselves are singing.
Monsters shake their arms
As if to say, "Beware! Danger! Go away!"
Then they disappear
And tall trees take their place.
Coarse grass shines ginger in the sun,
Reminding me of old men's beards.
The blades quiver,
Playing 'Simon Says' with their shadows.
A speck of red on a waving blade,
A ladybird,
Makes her way to nowhere.
Then slides down
And starts the journey up again.

Leila Anani (11)
Debenham High School
Stowmarket, Suffolk

Snake

Its blue bands,
Like varicose veins
On an old woman's legs,
Mingle with ageing armour . . .
Watercolour on an artist's canvas.
Forked tongue
Springs out of clamp mouth,
Like a trap door spider from its hidden home,
To taste the sweet Spring air.
Its jet black, lifeless eyes
Are the minute dots
On my Grandma's Tudor wall clock.
Dry, unmoisturised skin
Interlocks over tender flesh.
And yet he is a perfect killing machine
With his dislocating jaw . . .
Prey gone in a gulp
As he weaves his way
Through cooling rocks
Until his blue bands disappear
Into warm undergrowth.

Katrina Ann Clouting (13)
Halesworth Middle School
Halesworth, Suffolk

Who will go first?

We'll go first, said the ants
Because we are the smallest.

No, I'll go first, said Elephant
Because I'm the heaviest.

Sorry, but I'll go first, said the
Monkey.

No, said Noah
Giraffe is first, because his neck
has been hurting.

Kevin Horton (7)
Castleton C.P. School
Whitby, North Yorks
(Age Category Winner)

Animals animals

Cats have fur
Dogs have tails
Ladybirds have spots
Like chicken pox.

Pigs have snouts
Monkeys swing
Sheep go ba ba
like babies wa wa

Camels have humps
Elephants have trunks
Squirrels climb trees
so fast leaves go
crunch crunch crunch

Helen Reed (7)
Shirley, Solihull

Pig

The pig is a tank,
Slow, lumbering and tough skinned.
They come off the production line
Pink, squirming and already shuffling towards mother's
  teats.
I doubt they have any choice in the matter;
Their natural instinct compels them forward.

The pig is a JCB,
Emerging from the warmth and protection of the old sow
To dig the earth with rooting snout.

He seeks the roots and bulbs and, with luck, truffles.
Like gold dust to man,
And unforgettable delicacy to pig.

The pig is a submarine,
Waiting to sit down, sink down
In good, rich, dark, soft mud.
Up periscope!
A muddy, grinning face appears . . .
Just making sure he's not missing out on what the day
    might bring.

The pig is a mischievous schoolboy,
Grinning devilishly at you from ear to ear,
Charging about his field,
Larded in rich dark mud,
As he tries to outdo his fellows
In a pig olympics.

The pig is, sadly, a pork pie.
This noble beast, so much denounced
In phrases like: "Your bedroom is a pig sty"
And, "You eat like a pig",
Ends in the ultimate indignity of death . . .
Sitting on man's table,
A rosy apple in his mouth.

Gavin Bones (11)
Halesworth Middle School
Halesworth, Suffolk

The runt

His birth was troublesome.
It was February and bitterly cold.
Icicles, like daggers, hung off the barn doors.
A cold north wind blew.
It stung and whipped like dune grass.
He was number thirteen, unlucky.
There was no warm comforting straw.
It was bare hard concrete.
There was no life-giving milk,
Without a battle.
It was the cold shoulder for the runt . . .
Nothing was free, not even his mother's love.
And that wasn't true, pure love.
His piggy eyes bore the look of an outcast.
He was bruised,
Where his siblings had kicked him.
His chances were not great,
No wonder he died . . .
And we found him,
Stretched out in his pen.

Daniel Ribenfors (12)
Halesworth Middle School
Halesworth, Suffolk

THE BLACK CAT IS PATIENT

Poems about friendship and love

When I learned to walk

When I learned to walk
It was usually 1 step 2 step, Bonk
1 step 2 step, Bonk.
So I crawled instead.

When I learned to walk
It was usually 1 step 2 step, Bonk.
Until a friend came along —
Then it was 1 step 2 step 3 step.

Elizabeth Sears (10)
Newton County Primary School
Newton, Chester

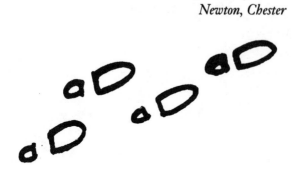

Friends

Friends are heart menders
Welding patches
Armed with a smile and a pair of ears
Others are traitors
Heartless liars
Breaking not mending
Armed with a rumour and a frown
Taking menders
And tearing out the nice warm smile
Sticking on a frown
Lodging the rumour into their brain
Then taking that rumour, like a virus,
And spreading it,
Smearing it,
All over the school
But some can resist the virus
With no medicine
That — is a true friend

Dominic McCaskill (10)
Allestree, Derby

Friend

She stands there on the doorstep
and hurls me back in time:

We ran out into the garden
and the clouds nestled down close
to hear the enchanted secrets we whispered
and left, forgotten, in the wind.
We danced underneath the sprinkler,
grasping each other's trembling fingers —
our small bodies spinning until we cried;
tears of laughter mingled with sparkling droplets
which made us tingle with cold;
we buried ourselves in comforting towels
and lay side by side in the ocean of grass.

The tears of laughter distil
into the disappearing years
which ran down our faces unnoticed.

I soak in her appearance —
her face has aged and changed.
She smiles. I know she feels it too.
Somewhere we are still dancing.

Rosanne Flynn (14)
North London
(Poet of the Year)

Warfare

I was Montgomery;
The snow was my desert sand.
I walked,
Snowball grenade held high.
My eyes squinted under the sun's deadly rays.
A movement?
Khaki against yellow?
No,
Black against white.
The grenade plotted its course.
A red-faced figure approached,
Rommel, my arch enemy.
He launched a counter attack
Which exploded on target.
Shells were exchanged all day.
He surrendered at dusk.
Where is he now,
The boy I called Rommel?

Neil Fordham (15)
Debenham High School
Stowmarket, Suffolk
(Age Category Winner)

Remember

Remember when we were little?
We were inseparable.
We stole the air from laughing at our jokes,
And crying from our grazed knees.
We played so much, we knew every game,
Except one.
Together in class, a world of our own.
The years grew on us.
Sometimes our world had wars.
But the dove always flew overhead.
We're learning the best game, life.
We still haven't finished it.
We've learnt the rules together,
We know them, and each other's.
We'll reach the last square together,
On the wings of our dove.
Hello you, Hello me.

Rosie Irvine (14)
Hove, East Sussex

Disaster

I'm not going to talk on a global scale,
But personal, when a friendship fails,
And all the secrets that you had shared,
Get spread around, like no-one cared,
The feelings about someone who you care for,
Get giggled at as you walk through the door,
And the person you confided in,
Sits at the back, grinning.

Jonathan Clarke (14)
Cefn Hengoed Comprehensive
Winchwen, Swansea

Love

Hiding in the shadows,
Lurking in the dark,
The black cat is patient
Waiting for its chance.

Its green eyes glitter
And then we feel its stare;
We are unassuming
And very unaware.

Is love not like this?
Is this not the way?
Is the black cat not our love
And we are all love's prey?

We know not when it starts
Or how it is born,
But at its arrival
It's like the Sun at dawn.

Laura Galbraith (15)
Queenswood School
Hatfield, Herts

Love poems

He's the brandy in the
Christmas Cake,
The seasoning in each
dish I bake
Although I'd sometimes love
to clout him
I can't imagine life
without him.

Love is:
The ache in my heart
the flutters in my stomach
The jelly in my legs
The shivers down my spine.

Amy Rogers (15)
Mortimer Wilson School
Alfreton, Derbyshire

What is this thing called love?

What is this love?
What is this thing
that makes us happy
makes us sing
makes us sad
makes us cry
and sometimes
makes us want to die
untangible, invisible?

What is this driving force
seems to be unending
seems to have no source?

Sean Cant (10)
North Crescent Primary School
Wickford, Essex

Futile obsessions

Her body — slender, delicate, divine;
But I can never feel its warmth.

Her eyes, serene, shining stars;
But they can never bestow that sparkle I yearn.

Her hair, a waterfall of golden streams;
But I can never feel their flow.

Her voice, a soft, melodious dream;
But it can never sing "I love you".

Her aroma, truly Heaven-scent;
Appreciated, but only from a distance.

Her hands, cushions of smooth silk;
But they can never touch mine.

Her mind, deep, thoughtful. She knows all, sees all;
But is blind to my longing for her.

She knows of my day-to-day love for her;
But of this truly deep desire She can never know.

She is far away now, the world lies between us;
But still I'm obsessed . . .

She is perfect in every way, a Goddess of Heaven;
And I am an invisible mortal in love, in hell.

Jamie Burke (16)
Ballyclare High School
Ballyclare

Her, me

Raindrops race down the window,
Fighting to reach the bottom,
Like I fight for her attention,
Every neutral glance,
Every passive word,
Means something to me.

Appreciation,
Apathy.
Understanding,
A closed mind.
Her,
Me.

Be yourself, they all say,
They don't understand,
I speak to her, tryng to impress,
But my speech becomes babbled,
Words mutilated,
Phrases devastated.

Love,
Indifference.
Attention,
Neglect.
Her,
Me.

"There's plenty more fish in the sea",
They say.
Correct, but there's many sharks too,
They don't realise, there's only one fish for me,
But to catch it, I'll probably drown.

Irritation,
Patience.
Condemnation,
Devotion.
Her,
Me.

Matthew Ringer (16)
Thorpe St Andrew School
Norwich

I REMEMBER THE DAY

Poems of time past

Playgroup Memory

That morning,
The blue smocked dress,
The dreaded dress,
The photograph dress
Appeared.
I sat.
The black box stared at me.
Its cold glass eye
Frightened me,
Stood between my mum and me.
Mum waved,
Laughed,
All for one smile.
I had become
Fragile,
Precious.
My lip trembled.
I sniffed.
The tears fell,
Running,
Falling on my hated dress.
Mum angrily held me,
Dried my eyes,
Put me on the seat.
Click.

In the photograph
I see the remains of tears
Caught in my eyes.

Francesca Wood (14)
Debenham High School
Stowmarket, Suffolk

Duck's day

It was spring
That's why a duck was flying in the wind.
I pulled out my gun
The time I took up
Meant he was gone.
Then I saw him again
He was flying towards the church.
My target and the trigger set
But someone lit a fire
Up flew the bird
The smoke blocked out my sight.

I ran home knowing
The duck had won the day.

Elliott Deakin (12)
Brightlands School
Glos

Harris fox

Upon the desolate rocks and grasses,
Of Harris' lonely hills,
The bare, dry body of a fox lies.
Its skin and flesh exiled long ago.
So it just lies
In its cave,
Empty eyes staring out,
Observing silently the world before it.
Watching over the seals,
The crabs,
The beautiful loch,
The distant croft all alone.
But somehow,
Unintentionally,
Creating an atmosphere around it so uneasy,
That when I discovered it,
I did not sleep for days.

Nicholas Pugh (12)
Bath, Avon
(Age Category Winner)

Climbing

That tree —
I remember,
The one with the lichen-green bark,
Dirty yellow leaves
And the owl hole at the top.
I remember —
The one we climbed
In the summer.
I remember
We snapped the thin branches
When they got in the way.
But now
The branches are thick,
Too thick to snap off.
We can't choose our path;
We have to make do.

Matthew Hart (14)
Debenham High School
Stowmarket, Suffolk

I remember the day

I loved to cuddle up
Against his smooth,
Soft fur.
And to hear his
Tail thumping the
Floor. His tummy steadily
Heaving in and out,
And his tongue licking
My face.
But now he's gone,
Gone forever.

We would take him for a
Walk in a field.
When we let him off
The lead he would
Chase every rabbit
In sight and rouse
Every bird. Mummy
Would call "Flipper." He
Bounded back and
Almost knocked us over.
But now he's not here,
And he can't come back.

Olivia Heal (10)
Beeston Hall School
West Runton, Cromer

My little brother

I shall never forget the day when my mother
gave birth to another.
I shall never forget when he'd just turned four
He was able to reach, to open the door.
I shall never forget when he started school
and he swam with arm-bands in the local pool.
I shall never forget when he turned nine,
He had the old school bag that used to be mine.
I shall never forget when he started middle,
It was then I realised he was not so little.
I shall never forget when he brought a friend home,
It was a girl, and her name was Simone.
I shall never forget when he turned thirteen,
He was fishing one day and he fell in the stream.
I shall never forget when he became a young man,
He was definitely no longer my mum's little lamb.
I shall never forget when he got a wife,
and I realised it was the start of his life!

Amie Foot (12)
Stowmarket, Suffolk

Remembering

As I shut my eyes
In a dark room
Thoughts buzz around my head
And I remember,
I remember my uncle.

Dark eyebrows
Two twinkling eyes
And a kind smile.
Just small things
That come together
To make a picture
That floats around my head.

Then the thought is broken
But something reminds me —
I think of his clothes
His old trousers
And woollen jumpers.
I could tell him anything.
He told me things over dinner

Things that made me laugh.
I miss him a lot.

Not in prison, not in heaven.
Just somewhere I cannot see him.

Kate Smith (10)
Landscove C. of E. Primary School
Newton Abbot, Devon
(Roald Dahl Wondercrump School Award)

Visiting Grannie

When we went to visit Grannie
At her old house near the shops,
We giggled at her purple hair
And baggy, dusty tights.
Sitting round the table,
We chuckled at the way
Grannie spat when eating,
As she talked about the war.
When we saw her in the street,
She looked so like a sheep,
Frail, and shyly grazing
Close by the Oxfam shop.
We pretended not to know her
As she hobbled up the road

Unless we needed money
And then we'd wave and shout.
We used to find it funny —
Her bolts at every door.
If strangers rang the doorbell,
She'd hiss and shoo them off.

When we went to visit Grannie
At the graveyard near the lake,
We cried for the way we'd laughed at her
When she was old and we were young.

Emily Sands (13)
Debenham High School
Stowmarket, Suffolk

Great Grandad

I used to visit Great Grandad four times a year.
And it was brilliant.
A sweaty yellow rope held up his trousers
And his black nylon moustache was trapped with bacon
  fat.
There were wet brown tea-bags on the sideboard near the
  sugar bowl
And rusty fish hooks stuck with dried worms.
He took me down to the cellar . . .
It was full of empty darkness, whispering with the sound of
  sea.
He came to a cupboard
And opened it with bent fingers.
He brought out his shiny medals . . .
"Now you can't get better than that, Sonny Jim!"
And he walked me up the dark cellar steps,
With medals in his hand.

Mark Grove (12)
Halesworth Middle School
Halesworth, Suffolk

Ivy

Ivy liked her fags, her wrestling and the cat,
in fact the cat ate better than her.
Her hair had a blond streak at the front of her head,
this is where the nicotine had settled.

The fag hung from the corner of her mouth,
at 89 she must be a tough old bird.
She couldn't hear things at all well
but only the cat meow.

She'd yell at the telly when the wrestling was on,
"COME ON COME ON YOU BLOODY LOT!"
the goody would win and the baddie would lose,
and the TV she then switched off.

Ivy ate pigs' tails most dinner times,
sucking it because of her lack of teeth.
She could roll her false teeth around and around
and stick her tongue through the gap.

Hannah Gregory (17)
John Bentley School
Calne, Wilts

The mining days

The black, looming outline of the pit wheel.
Through the smothering mist,
Like a giant on the horizon.
Down the giant's open mouth,
Sitting on a piece of wood,
Going down on a rusty, clanging chain.
At the end of my endless journey down,
Walking to the coal face,
The dim light of candles
Casting shadows on the black, scowling wall.
Picks striking.
Echoes all around.
Then up the chain.
Down the road, homeward bound.
Once, when I was a child.

Once down the shaft
The black giant laughed
proclaiming certain death.
Ponies trotting through the unearthly silence.
Then the deafening explosion of dynamite.
The raging fire.

Further down the pit
Screams and shouts from all about.
The once peaceful mine in uproar
Then it lay rusting desolate and dead.
Once, when I was a child.

Amy Jones (12)
Bryncoch Church in Wales Primary School
Neath, West Glamorgan

THE BLACK SKY DRAGON

DRAGON

Poems of the imagination

If I was Princess Diana

If I was Princess Diana
I could hold a banner
and with my best friend Hannah
We could play the piana.

I would put on my brooch
and get in my coach.
I went to see the Queen
but she was really mean.

So I went to see the King
and he gave me a ring.

Perhaps I should be me
and see
How it turns out to be.

Vanessa Rinaldi (7)
St Mary's School
Thornbury, Bristol

Scissors

Mother's cutting up material.
She sees scissors, I don't.
I see Siamese twins, trying to escape
and run from each other.
Mother sees scissors, I don't.
I see Mother and child back to back,
standing as part of one another, lovingly.
Mother sees scissors, I don't.
I see a toucan, beak and all,
all eyes peering, glaring at me viciously.
Mother sees scissors, I don't.
I see a palm leaf, hanging beneath two coconuts.
A small insect, searching upon it.
Mother sees scissors, I don't.

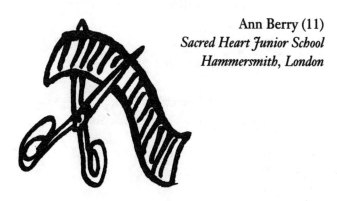

Ann Berry (11)
Sacred Heart Junior School
Hammersmith, London

Repentance To An Elephant

The Elephant sat on me
As if to say "naughty"
I promised I wouldn't do it again
But the galaxy doesn't
Revolve around logic
So the Elephant pressed
I confessed my wicked desires
Repented
And was duly released
But then I noticed fences
Growing all around me
And high stone walls
Large and scaling
So I ran away
As fast as I could
In search of another girl

Christopher Bishop (17)
Hampstead School
London

The box

In my mind is a big, cardboard box
Which has colours on it.

The lid opens slowly
With a banging and hissing sound.
The inside is covered with glass spikes.
A green grasshopper hops about
With its long green feelers
Touching the bottom of the box.
It comes hopping out
And leaps through the open door
On to the lawn.

The perfume of strawberry soap
Rises gently and floats away.

A dream about fairies
Comes out with a woosh
And it flies over two fields
to land in the woods.

There is a happy witch's laugh
Which gurgles out of the box
And into the far-away distance.

The box has a worry.
It is that the witch is still inside
And the box thinks
She is going to put a spell on it
And the lid closes with a crash
And the witch
Explodes.

Hugo Denby-Mann (6)
Horler's Pre-preparatory School
Comberton, Cambridge

Toys

What do you think happens in your bedroom at night?
I know what happens in mine . . .
My teddies come out and stamp on my clothes
And my robot wakes up and joins in
My soldier marches through my cupboards
Trying to wake up all the others.
Paper and paint, pencils and rubbers
Jump around in a box, and THAT wakes up the others.
"Bang Bang" — they're making a noise
But when I wake up, it STOPS!

Sean Casey (8)
Upper Wortley Primary School
Leeds

Dreams

On a cold winter's eve
At the stroke of midnight.
A prince was asleep
And dreamed of a golden castle.
A farmer was asleep
And dreamed of a field of golden vegetables.
My mum was asleep
And dreamed of all the washing done for her for a year.
A dog was asleep
And dreamed of a juicy bone.
Helen my friend was asleep
And dreamed of her best friend coming to England.
A skunk was asleep
And dreamed of not smelling.
A chair was asleep
And dreamed of people not sitting on it.
A fairy was asleep
And dreamed of not pulling children's teeth out.
I was asleep
and dreamed of being able to swim.

Krishna Mistry (7)
Heathfield School
Pinner

Spooky poem

Skeletons give me a fright
On a misty night
Ugly monsters give me the creeps
When I'm in bed, fast asleep
Ghastly ghosts, all white
Are a terrifying sight
A witch zooming on her broom
Scares me in my bedroom
In my bed
Here I dread
The sleeping dead . . .

Mark Gillah (7)
Parsons Down Junior School
Thatcham, Berks

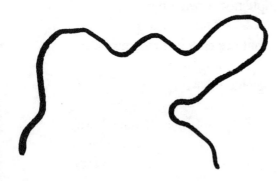

The staircase ghost

I met a ghost upon the stairs,
A ghost which caught me unawares.
I could not believe my eyes,
It was of such a massive size.
I thought ghosts were white as sheets
But this was the weirdest I ever did meet.
Its height, I think, was ten foot two,
From bowler hat to blackened shoe.
I put out my hand for him to shake,
But then he said "For goodness sake,
We don't need handshakes and all that,
My name is Jeremiah Pratt,
Once the tallest man in the world,
My story will now be unfurled.
I hit my head on a passing plane
I'll never feel quite the same again."
Then he vanished without a word,
Before I could check that I hadn't misheard.
I thought no more of my visitor,
I am no inquisitor,
But it goes to show that ghosts are there,
You could meet one anywhere.

Robert Davies (10)
University College School
Hampstead, London

The Black Sky dragon

The Black Sky Dragon with children following close
Was weaving his way around the great sky dome
The moon falling lower, turning into a black cloud
One sparkling star above one special tree
Black clouds turning darker and darker
Trees moving into the shape of a monster

Hannah Roche (7)
Wincanton, Somerset

Pirate vessel

A black and ragged, threadbare flag,
A sail patched with coloured rags.
A tarnished deck of amber and red,
A majestic dragon at her head.
A deserted black and eerie hold,
Which used to be furnished with silver and gold.
Moored in the port from evening to dawn,
When foaming white horses ride in a storm.
Or when soft golden ripples dance in the sun,
Looking to sea where the otters have swum.

Francisca Wiggins (9)
Heathlands Preparatory School
Grantham

Cassandra

Breathing the musty air of the temple,
The blinding darkness engulfs her.
Slender, pale hands cleanse a bright golden bowl,
Pour water,
Again and again,
Wash away the blood of a sacrifice.
Her voice rises,
Filling the chamber with an ancient call
To an ancient god.
Her lips barely move: cursed lips,
Never to be trusted.
Apollo's possession,
Apollo's priestess,
Apollo's virgin bride.
As suddenly as it began, her song ends.
Her ears strain,
And recognise the sound of burning,
A screaming child,
A soldier in pain,
A warrior's cry to battle,
A mother's grieving wail as she weaves a shroud for her
    son.
Death is blown,
Like transparent dandelion seeds on a breeze, through the
    city.

Troy is falling.
Precious, precious Troy.
Greece is the plague,
The Greeks avenge beautiful Helen, bewitching Helen.

Chloe Williams (14)
Leamington Spa, Warks

Ichabad inkerman mungo-varadi

The letterbox clattered. She ran downstairs,
With only one sock on and rubbing her eyes,
Hair half brushed and a bowl of cornflakes
In her hand, dripping milk.

"Mum, get that telephone please," she yelled
As it shrilled through the house.
She picked up the letter. One letter,
In a plain white envelope.

Ripping open the top a note fell out.
She turned it over. All it said was,
"Ichabad inkerman mungo-varadi."
What does it mean?

Before there was time to wonder,
Her mother called, "It's for you."
She took the phone from the outstretched hand
And held it to her ear.

A voice, so soft she could hardly hear,
Whispered like a breeze at her.
"Ichabad inkerman mungo-varadi."
The phone dropped.

An idea forming in her head
She ran to Sally's house — obvious!
It was her friends playing a joke,
She saw them laughing in the window.

She knocked on the door — no answer —
And pushed. It creaked inwards,
"Sally . . . Tom?" Silent as a grave.
She gingerly entered the living room.

They turned, she saw their faces,
As white as the paper through her door,
Together, in voices as cold as ice, they said:
"Ichabad inkerman mungo-varadi."

She screamed and ran, to next-door's garden,
Crouched behind the dustbin, hiding,
And the dog on the doorstep turned and growled
"Ichabad inkerman mungo-varadi."

She backed away towards the gate,
Something ghastly white touched her arm,
And she froze as though she had been painted
White from head to toe.

Sally's small brother, passes the gate,
"Hazel — what's wrong with Sally?"
She opens her mouth with teeth like icicles,
"Ichabad inkerman mungo-varadi."

Jessica Matthews (12)
Ovingham Middle School
Ovingham, Northumberland

LAST WORD

The field mouse

I looked at my blank page —
And saw her —
Falling from a wheat sheaf
To the ground with a soft thud.

I saw her smooth, silky fur
Over the delicate, fragile bones,
Her innocent hazelnut eyes,
And little pink nose.

A faint smell of earth,
Hay, straw and cornflour,
Winding its way
Into my head.

The sound of scuffling
And nervousness reached my ears . . .
Then — I blinked, and she was gone
My poem lay before me.

Eleanor Collins (11)
Bozeat, Northants

Index of Titles

Index of Poets